The Way of Holiness

With Notes by the Way; Being a Narrative of Experience Resulting from a Determination to Be a Bible Christian

By Phoebe Palmer

Published by Pantianos Classics

ISBN-13: 978-1-78987-527-0

First published in 1843

Contents

Dedication .... *iv*

Introduction .... *v*

Preface to Second Edition .... *vi*

Chapter One - Is There Not A Shorter Way? 8

Chapter Two 10

Chapter Three 11

Chapter Four 13

Chapter Five 14

Chapter Six 17

Chapter Seven 19

Chapter Eight - There Is But One Way 23

Chapter Nine 25

Notes by the Way 31

Chapter One 31

Chapter Two 34

Chapter Three 35

Chapter Four 37

Chapter Five 41

Chapter Six 43

Chapter Seven 46

Chapter Eight 49

Dedication

Affectionately Inscribed

To My

Beloved and Honored Parents

In Token Of Grateful Remembrance

Of the religious culture so assiduously bestowed during childhood,
and the Judicious counsel and sympathy of riper years,
with the fervent prayer,
that they through Whose instrumentality,
"I from a child have Known the Scriptures," and who may make rapid
advancement in the
"Way of Holiness during life, and who shall have, eventually, an abundant
entrance ministered unto them
into the everlasting kingdom of our Lord and Savior,
Jesus Christ.

The Author

Introduction

Who has not been charmed and instructed by Travel and "Incidents of Travel" in the "Holy Land" — India — Europe — America, &c.? Travelers of every variety of talent, almost from time immemorial, have transmitted through the press the result of journeyings and patient investigation. What has not been narrated by one, whose genius might have instigated him to particularize elaborately on the topic suited to his peculiar cast of mind, has been pictured by another, signalized for a species of investigation unthought of by his predecessor, till information suited to every grade of intellect has been so fully given, that firmness is requisite to bear up against the impression, that public sentiment may not label a new production with "thirst for book-making," "egotism" and the like.

Not so with the traveler to the heavenly city. A field of investigation, boundless as eternity, is before him. Earth hath its boundaries; but the inquiring, insatiate spirit of the heavenly traveler, is nowhere, in all his onward journeying, met with the interdict, "Hitherto shalt thou come, but no further." No! the inspiring insignia is blazoned at every progressive point in his pilgrimage, "Then shall ye know, if ye follow on to know."

And yet it should not be forgotten that an enemy, subtle beyond all human conception, doth, with all his malicious agencies,

---"his march oppose,"

and is ever lurking about his heavenward way ready with well-circumstanced devices to with stand every step of an onward course. In view of such considerations, the Christian public will not deem an apology necessary for presenting a narrative of journeyings in the "Way of Holiness, with Notes by the Way."

It will be observed, throughout, that with this traveler, the BIBLE was the all-commanding chart by which the propriety of each successive step was determined, and the work is now sent forth to the world, with the fervent prayer that its perusal may be helpful toward inspiring the reader with more confirmed views of the infinite importance and excellency of the Scriptures.

Preface to Second Edition

For the kindness with which the first edition of this little volume has been received, the author acknowledges herself under obligation to the Christian public. She regards it as no small favor that the mantle of charity has been thrown over its imperfections, and its humble aim to guide the sincere seeker into the way of holiness, not wholly unanswered. A desire to present entire consecration as a duty enjoined in the Scriptures, and not merely the peculiarity of a sect, induced the author, before issuing the first edition to query, whether the volume should be entitled "Bible Christianity," or "The Way of Holiness." The latter was decided upon, from the consideration that the Bible presents but *one* way to heaven, and that, "The *Way* of Holiness." But from the encouragements received from gentlemen of different evangelical churches, she, with gratitude to God, acknowledges the fact, that her aim to present "Bible Christianity" has not been unsuccessful. For the satisfaction of those unacquainted with its doctrinal Sentiments, it has been thought advisable to subjoin two or three testimonials from individuals who stand forth before the Christian public as honorable advocates of Bible religion.

By the Rev. President Mahan, Congregational Minister

Next in value to the grace of God in the heart, and to the word of life in which that grace is revealed, is a precious book that throws light on the way of holiness, and, with all the warmth and force of light and love, enters upon the business of leading the soul to God. The reading of such a book is an era in the life of an inquirer after the great salvation. We noted down the above thoughts after an attentive perusal of a little work under the title placed at the head of this article. We regard the reading of this book as an era in the progress of our Christian experience. So it is regarded by- numbers who have read it in this place. We recommend it as one of the best books that can be placed in the hands of inquirers after full salvation in Christ. *It bears the stamp of no one particular sect!* but teaches the way of holiness in truth and love. We wish that those who oppose the doctrine of holiness would read this book, and then ask themselves whether that doctrine really tends to let down, as has been reported, the standard of the gospel, and whether such a state of experience can originate from dangerous error, or from any other than the Spirit of truth! – Oberlin Evangelist.

By the Rev. L. L. Hamline, A. M. [1]

We do not expect our female readers to buy and peruse every book mentioned in these notices, but here is one which we are not willing to suppose will escape the examination of any Christian woman whose eye may light upon this recommendation of it. Of all that has been written on the blessed theme of entire sanctification, it is doubtful if anything is better calculated than this to rouse pious desire, and guide the soul in its seeking. There is an unusual degree of simplicity in the narrative, such as we think could not be arrived at, except by the chastening power of the Sanctifier. The author has but one aim, namely, to present pictures - Daguerreotype impressions – of her states of mind, from the time she started in the way to seek holiness, until, and after she attained it. The difficulties she encountered – their effect upon her mind – and the manner of her escape, are all so represented that the pious reader readily apprehends them, and often finds that as in water, face answereth to face, so does heart to heart, in religious experience. We earnestly commend this little volume to all who hunger and thirst after righteousness.
Ladies' Repository

[1] Now one of the bishops of the M. E. Church.

Chapter One - Is There Not A Shorter Way?

"Be always ready to give an answer to every man that asketh you a reason of the hope that is within you, with meekness and fear." — Peter

"I have thought," said one of the children of Zion to the other, as in love they journeyed onward in the way cast up for the ransomed of the Lord to walk in; "I have thought," said he, "whether there is not a *shorter way* of getting into this way of holiness than some of our brethren apprehend?"

"Yes," said the sister addressed, who was a member of the denomination alluded to; "Yes, brother, there is a shorter way! O! I am sure this long waiting and struggling with the powers of darkness is not necessary. There is a shorter way." And then, with a solemn feeling of responsibility, and with a realizing conviction of the truth uttered, she added, "But, brother, there is but one way."

Days and even weeks elapsed, and yet the question, with solemn bearing, rested upon the mind of that sister. She thought of the affirmative given in answer to the inquiry of the brother — examined yet more closely the Scriptural foundation upon which the truth of the affirmation rested — and the result of the investigation lended to add still greater confirmation to the belief, that many sincere disciples of Jesus, by various needless perplexities, consume much time in endeavoring to get into this way, which might, more advantageously to themselves and others, be employed in making progress in it, and testifying, from experimental knowledge, of its blessedness.

How many, whom Infinite Love would long since have brought into this state, instead of seeking to be brought into the possession of the blessing at once, are seeking a preparation for the reception of it! They feel that their Convictions are not deep enough to warrant an approach to the throne of grace, with the confident expectation of receiving the blessing now. Just at this point some may have been lingering months and years. Thus did the sister, who so confidently affirmed "there is a shorter way." And here, dear child of Jesus, permit the writer to tell you just how that sister found the "shorter way."

On looking at the requirements of the word of God, she beheld the command, "Be ye holy." She then began to say in her heart, "Whatever my former deficiencies may have been, God requires that I should *now* be holy. Whether *convicted*, or otherwise, *duty is plain*. God requires present holiness." On coming to this point, she at once apprehended a simple truth before unthought of, *i.e.*, *Knowledge is conviction*. She well knew that, for along time, she had been assured that God required holiness. But she had never deemed this knowledge a sufficient plea to take to God — and because of present need, to ask a present bestowment of the gift.

Convinced that in this respect she had mistaken the path, she now, with renewed energy, began to make use of the knowledge already received, and to discern a "shorter way."

Another difficulty by which her course had been delayed she found to be here. She had been accustomed to look at the blessing of holiness as such a high attainment, that her general habit of soul inclined her to think it almost beyond her reach. This erroneous impression rather influenced her to rest the matter thus:— "I will let every high state of grace, in name, alone, and seek only to be *fully conformed to the will of God, as recorded in his written word.* My chief endeavors shall be centered in the aim to be an humble Bible Christian. By the grace of God, all my energies shall be directed to this one point. With this single aim, I will journey onward, even though my faith may be tried to the uttermost by those manifestations being withheld, which have previously been regarded as essential for the establishment of faith."

On arriving at this point, she was enabled to gain yet clearer insight into the simplicity of the way. And it was by this process. After having taken the Bible as the rule of life, instead of the opinions and experience of professors, she found, on taking the blessed word more closely to the companionship of her heart, that no one declaration spoke more appealingly to her understanding than this: "Ye are not your own, ye are bought with a price, therefore glorify God in your body and spirit which are his."

By this she perceived the duty of entire consecration in a stronger light, and as more sacredly binding, than ever before. Here she saw God as her Redeemer claiming by virtue of the great price once paid for the redemption of body, soul and spirit the *present and entire service* of all these redeemed powers.

By this she saw that if she lived constantly in the entire surrender of all that had been thus dearly purchased unto God, she was but an unprofitable servant; and that, if less than all was rendered, she was worse than unprofitable, inasmuch as she would be guilty of keeping back part of that price which had been purchased unto God: "Not with corruptible things, such as silver and gold, but by the precious blood of Jesus." And after so clearly discerning the will of God concerning her, she felt that the sin of Ananias and Sapphira would be less culpable in the sight of Heaven than her own, should she not at once resolve on living in the entire consecration of all her redeemed powers God.

Deeply conscious of past unfaithfulness, she now determined that the time past should suffice; and with a humility of spirit, induced by a consciousness of not having lived in the performance of such a "reasonable service," she was enabled, through grace, to resolve, with firmness of purpose, that entire devotion of heart and life to God should be the absorbing subject of the succeeding pilgrimage of life.

Chapter Two

"We by his Spirit prove,
And know the things of God,
The things which freely of his love
He hath on us bestow'd."

After having thus resolved on devoting the entire service of her heart and life to God, the following questions occasioned much serious solicitude:— How shall I know when I have consecrated all to God? And whether God *accepts* the sacrifice — and how know the manner of its acceptance? Here again the blessed Bible, which she had now taken as her counselor, said to her heart, "We have received not the spirit of the world, but the Spirit which is of God, that we might know the things freely given to us of God."

It was thus she became assured that it was her privilege to *know when she* had consecrated all to God, and also to know that the sacrifice was *accepted,* and the resolve was solemnly made that the subject should not cease to be absorbing, until this knowledge was obtained.

Feeling it a matter of no small importance to stand thus solemnly pledged to God, conscious that sacred responsibilities were included in these engagements, a *realization* of the fact, that neither body, soul, nor spirit, time, talent, nor influence, were, even for one moment, at her own disposal, began to assume the tangibility of living truth to her mind, in a manner not before apprehended.

From a sense of responsibility thus imposed, she began to be more abundant in labors, "instant in season and out of season."

While thus engaged in active service, another difficulty presented itself. How much of self in these performances? said the accuser. For a moment, almost bewildered at being thus withstood, her heart began to sink. She felt most keenly that she had no certain standard to raise up against this accusation?

It was here again that the blessed word sweetly communed with her heart, presenting the marks of the way, by a reference to the admonition of Paul: "Therefore, my beloved brethren, be ye steadfast and unmovable, always abounding in the work of the Lord, forasmuch as ye know that your labor is not in vain in the Lord."

These blessed communings continued thus: If the primitive Christians had the assurance that their labors were in the Lord; and then enjoyed the heart-inspiring *confidence* that their labors were *not in vain,* because performed in the might of the Spirit, then it is also your privilege to know that your labor is in the Lord.

It was at this point in her experience that she first perceived the *necessity,* and also the *attainableness* of the witness of *purity of intention* which, in her petition to God, as most expressive of her peculiar need, she denominated, "The witness that the spring of every motive is pure."

It was by the Word of the Lord she became fully convinced that she needed this heart encouraging confidence in order to insure success in her labors of love. The next step taken was to resolve, as in the presence of the Lord, not to cease importuning the throne of grace until the witness was given "that the spring of every motive was pure."

On coming to this decision the blessed Word most encouragingly, yes, and also assuringly said to her heart "Stand Still, and see the salvation of God!"

Chapter Three

"Here, in thine own appointed way,
    I wait to learn thy will;
Silent I stand before thy face,
    And hear thee say, Be still!
Be still and know that I am God:
    'Tis all I wish to know,
To feel the virtue of thy blood,
    And spread its praise below."

Thus admonished, she began to anticipate, with longings unutterable, the fulfillment of the WORD upon which she had been enabled to rest her hope.

These exercises, though so deep as to assure the heart, most powerfully and permanently, that "the word of the Lord is quick and powerful, and sharper than any two-edged sword, piercing to the dividing asunder of the soul and spirit, and of the joints and marrow, and is a discerner of the thoughts and intents of the heart," were not of that distressing character which, according to her preconceived opinions, were necessary, preparatory to entering into a state of holiness.

So far from having those overwhelming perceptions of guilt, on which she afterward saw she had been too much disposed to place reliance, as somewhat meritorious, she was constantly and *consciously* growing in grace daily — yea, even hourly her heavenward progress seemed marked as by the finger of God.

No gloomy fears that she was *not a child of God* dimmed her spiritual horizon, presenting fearful anticipations of impending wrath. There had been a period in her experience, some time previous to that under present consideration, from which she had not *one lingering doubt of her acceptance with God, as a member of the household of faith. But, conscious that she had not the witness of entire consecration to God,* neither the assurance that the great deep of her heart, the fountain from whence action emanates, was pure, which at this time stood before the vision of her mind as two distinct objects, (yet which, as she afterward perceived, most clearly merged in *one,*) and impelled onward also by such an intense desire to be *fruitful in every good work*, the emotions of her spirit could not perhaps be more clearly expressed than in the nervous language of the poet:-

"My heart strings groan with deep complaint,
   My flesh lies panting, Lord, for thee;
And every limb, and every joint,
   Stretches for perfect purity."

And yet, to continue poetic language, it was "sweet distress," for the *word of the Lord* continually said to her heart, "The Spirit helpeth our infirmities;" and conscious that, she had submitted herself to the dictations of the Spirit, a sacred conviction took possession of her mind that she was being led into all truth.

"Stand still, and see the salvation of God," was now the listening attitude in which her soul eagerly waited before the Lord; and it was but a few hours after the above encouraging admonition had been spoken to her heart that she set apart a season to wait before the Lord, especially for the bestowment of the object, or rather the two distinct objects previously stated.

On first kneeling, she thought of resolving that she would continue to wait before the Lord until the desire of her heart was granted. But the adversary, who had stood ready to withstand every progressive step, suggested, "Be careful, God may disappoint your expectations; and suppose you should be left to wrestle all night; ay, and all the morrow too?"

She had ever felt it a matter of momentous import to say, either with the language of the heart or lip, "I have lifted my hand to God;" and for a moment she hesitated whether she should really determine to continue in a waiting attitude until the desire of her heart was fulfilled; but afterward concluded to rest the matter thus: One duty can never, in the order of God, interfere with another; and, unless necessarily called away by surrounding circumstances, I will, in the strength of grace wait till my heart is assured, though it may be all night, and all the morrow too.

And here most emphatically could she say, she was led by a "way she knew not;" so simple, so clearly described, and urged by the Word of the Lord, and yet so often overlooked, for want of that child-like simplicity which, without reasoning takes God at his word. It was just while engaged in the act of preparing the way, as she deemed, to some great and indefinable exercise, that the Lord, through the medium of faith in his written word, led her astonished soul directly into the "way of holiness," where, with unutterable delight, she found the comprehensive desires of her soul blended and satisfied in the fulfillment of the command, *"Be ye holy."*

It was thus, waiting child of Jesus, that this traveler in the King's highway was directed onward, through the teachings of the word of God, and induced so confidently to affirm, in reply to the brother, *"There is a shorter way."*

Chapter Four

Thou message from the skies!
  Ray for the rayless heart!
Thou fount of wisdom for the wise!
  A balm for all thou art.

Man of my counsel, thou!
  Blessings untold rejoice
The heart of those who meekly bow,
  To listen to thy voice.

It was on this wise that the *word of the Lord,* the "Book of books," as a "mighty counselor," urged her onward, and by unerring precept directed every step of the way. And as each progressive step by which she was ushered into the enjoyment of this blessed state of experience was as distinctly marked, by its holy teachings, as those already given, may it not be presumed, that some heretofore wavering one may be induced to rest more confidently in the assurance that "the word of the Lord is tried," and is the same in its immutable nature as the Faithful and True, by stating, as nearly as will comport with the brevity required, the steps as successively taken by which this disciple of Jesus entered?

Over and again, previous to the time mentioned, had she endeavored to give herself away in covenant to God. But she had never till this hour, deliberately resolved on counting the cost, with the solemn intention to "reckon herself dead *indeed* unto sin, but alive unto God through Jesus Christ our Lord;" to account herself permanently the Lord's, and in verity no more at her own disposal, but *irrevocably the Lord's property,* for time and eternity. Now, in the name of the Lord Jehovah, after having deliberately "counted the cost," she resolved to enter into the bonds of an everlasting covenant, with the fixed purpose to *count all things loss* for the excellency of the knowledge of Jesus, that she might know him and the power of his resurrection, by being made conformable to his death, and raised to an entire newness of life.

Apart from any excitement of feeling, other than the sacred awe inspired by the solemnity of the act, she now, in experimental verity, *did* lay hold upon the terms of the covenant, by which God has condescended to bind himself to his people, being willing, yea, even desirous, to bring down the responsibility of a perpetual engagement upon herself, even in the sight of heaven. So intensely was she desirous that earth should usurp a claim no more, she asked: that the solemn act might be recorded before the eternal throne, that the "host of the Lord that encamp round about them that fear him" might bear witness, and also the innumerable company of the redeemed, blood-washed spirits, should behold yet another added to their choir in spirit, and also in song; and though still a resident of earth, they should witness the ceaseless return of all her redeemed powers, *through Christ,* ascending as an acceptable sacrifice. The obligation to take the service of God as the absorbing business of life, and to regard heaven as her native home, and the accumulation of treasure in heaven the chief object of ambition, was at this solemn moment entered upon.

On doing this, a hallowed sense of consecration took possession of her soul; a divine conviction that the covenant was recognized in heaven, accompanied with the assurance that the seal, proclaiming, her wholly the Lord's, was set: while a consciousness, deep and abiding, that she had been but a co-worker with God in this matter, added still greater confirmation to her conceptions of the extent and permanency of those heaven-inspired exercises, by which a mighty work had been wrought in and for her soul, which she felt assured would tell on her eternal destiny, even after myriads of ages had been spent in the eternal world.

But she did not at the moment regard the state into which she had been brought as the "way of holiness," neither had the word holiness been the most prominent topic during this solemn transaction. *Conformity to the will of God in all things* was the absorbing desire of her heart. Yet after having passed through these exercises she began to give expression to her full soul thus: "I am wholly thine! -- Thou dost reign unrivaled in my heart! There is not a tie that binds me to earth; every tie has been severed, and now I am wholly, wholly thine!" While lingering on the last words, the Holy Spirit appealingly repeated the confident expressions to her heart, thus: What! wholly the Lord's? Is not this the holiness that God requires? What have you more to render? Does God require more than all? Hath he issued the command, "Be ye holy," and not given the ability, with the command, for the performance of it? Is he hard master, unreasonable in his requirements? She now saw, in a convincing light, her error in regarding holiness as an attainment beyond her reach, and stood reproved, though consciously shielded by the atonement from condemnation, and enjoying the blessedness of that soul "to whom the Lord will not impute sin."

And now the eyes of her understanding were more fully opened, and founded on eternal faithfulness did she find the words of the Savior, *"If any man will do his will he shall know of the doctrine."*

Chapter Five

"Let us, to perfect love restored,
   Thine image here retrieve,
And in the presence of our Lord
   The life of angels live.

"But is it possible that I
   Should live and sin no more?
Lord, if on thee I dare rely,
   The *faith shall bring the power.*"

She now saw that holiness, instead of being an attainment beyond her reach, was a state of grace in which every one of the Lord's redeemed ones should live — that the service was indeed a "reasonable service," inasmuch as the command; "Be ye holy," is founded upon the absolute right which God, as our Creator, Preserver, and Redeemer, has upon the entire service of his creatures.

Instead of perceiving anything meritorious in what she had been enabled, through grace, to do, that is, in laying all upon the altar, she saw that she had but rendered back to God that which was already his own.

She looked upon family, influence, earthly possessions, &c., and chidingly, in view of former misappropriation, said to her heart, "What hast thou, that thou hast not received? And if received, why didst thou glory in them as of thine own begetting?" And though with Abraham in the sacrifice of his beloved Isaac, she was called seemingly to sacrifice what was of all earthly objects surpassingly dear, yet so truly did she now see that the "Giver of every good gift" but rightfully required his own in his own time, that she could only say, "The Lord gave, and the Lord hath taken away, blessed be the name of the Lord."

And O, what cause for deep and perpetual abasement before God did she now perceive, in that she had so long kept back part of that price which, by the requirement of that blessed word, she now so clearly discerned infinite love had demanded! and when the inquiries were presented,

"Is God unreasonable in his requirements? Hath he given the command, 'Be ye holy,' and not given the ability, with the command, for the performance of it?" her inmost soul, penetrated with a sense of past unfaithfulness, acknowledged not only the reasonableness of the command, but also the unreasonableness of not having lived in obedience to such a plain Scriptural requirement.

With a depth of feeling not before experienced, she could now respond heartily to the sentiment,

"I loathe myself when Christ I see,
    And into nothing fall,
Content if God exalted be,
    And Christ be *all* in *all*."

Never before did she so deeply realize the truth of the words, "For we have received the sentence of death in ourselves, that we should not trust in ourselves, but in Him that raiseth the dead." With poverty of spirit her heart was constantly giving utterance to its emotions with the poet

"Thou all our works in us hast wrought,
    Our good is all divine,
The praise of every virtuous thought
    And righteous act is thine."

And when (as she still continued in a waiting attitude before the Lord) the Spirit appealed to her understanding thus, "Through what power have you been enabled thus to present yourself a living sacrifice to God?" her heart replied "Through the power of God. I could no more have brought myself, but through faith, in God, believing it to be his requirement, than I could have created a world!" Immediately the Spirit suggested, "If God has enabled you to bring it, will he not, now that you bring it and lay it on his altar, accept it at your hands?" She now, indeed, began to feel that all things were ready! and, in thrilling anticipation, began to say, "Thou *wilt* receive me! yes, *thou wilt receive me!*" And still she fell that something was wanting. "But when and how shall I know that thou *dost* receive me?" said the importunate language of her heart. The Spirit presented the declaration of the written word in reply, "Now is the accepted time." Still her insatiable desires were unsatisfied; and yet she continued to wait with unutterable importunity of desire and longing expectation, looking upward for the coming of the Lord; while the Spirit continued to urge the Scriptural declarations, "'*Now is the accepted time,*' *I will receive you*. Only believe! Trust all, *now* and *for ever,* upon the faithfulness of the IMMUTABLE WORD, and you are *now* and *for ever* the *saved* of the Lord!" And now an increase of light in reference to the sacredness and immutability of the word of God burst upon her soul! An assurance that the Holy Scripture is, in verity, the WORD OF THE LORD, and as immutable in its nature as the *throne of the Eternal,* assumed the vividness and vitality of TRUTH, in a manner that she had never before realized.

These views were given in answer to an inquiry that rose in her mind, thus — "Shall I *venture* upon these declarations without *previously* realizing a change sufficient to warrant such conclusions? Venture *now,* merely because they stand thus recorded in the *written word!* She here perceived that the declarations of Scripture were as truly the WORD OF THE LORD to her soul, as though they were proclaimed from the holy mount in the voice of thunder, or blazoned across the vault of heaven in characters of flame. She now saw into the simplicity of faith in a manner that astonished and humbled her soul; she was astonished she had not before perceived it, and humbled because she had been so slow of heart to believe God. The perceptions of faith and its effect that then took possession of her mind were these: *Faith is taking God at his word,* relying unwaveringly upon his truth. The nature of the truth believed, whether joyous or otherwise, will necessarily produce corresponding feeling. Yet, *faith* and *feeling* are two distinct objects, though so nearly allied.

Here she saw an error which, during the whole of her former pilgrimage in the heavenly way, had been detrimental to her progress. She now perceived that she had been much more solicitous about *feeling* than *faith* — requiring *feeling,* the *fruit* of faith, previous to having exercised faith.

And now, on discerning the way more clearly, she was enabled by the help of the Spirit to resolve that she *would take God at his word,* whatever her emotions might be. Here she was permitted to linger for a moment, to count the cost of living a life of faith on the Son of God. The question was presented, "Suppose after you have ventured upon the bare declaration of God — resolved to believe that a*s you venture upon his word he doth receive you just because* he hath said, 'I will receive you,' and then should perceive no change, no extraordinary evidence, or emotion, to confirm your faith, would you still believe?" The answer from the WORD was, *"The just shall live by faith."*

She now came to the decision that if called to live peculiarly the life of faith, and denied all outward or inward manifestations to an extent before unheard of, with the exception of him who "journeyed" onward in obedience to the command of "God, not knowing whither he went," she would still, through the power of the ALMIGHTY, who has said, *"Walk* before me, and be thou perfect," journey onward through the pilgrimage of life — *walking by faith* — resolved that the shield of faith should never be relinquished, but retained even with the unyielding grasp of death, should the powers of darkness be permitted to assail her thus formidably. Never can the important step that followed be forgotten in time or in eternity.

Chapter Six

"He staggered not at the promise of God through unbelief but was strong in faith, giving glory to God. being fully persuaded that what he had promised he was able also to perform." — *The word of God.*

"Faith in thy power thou seest I have,
   For thou this faith hast wrought,
Dead souls thou callest from the grave,
   And speakest worlds from naught.

"In hope against all human hope,
   Self-desperate, I believe,
Thy *quickening word shall raise me up,*
   Thou shalt thy Spirit give.

"The thing surpasses all my thought,
   But faithful is my Lord:
Through unbelief I stagger not,
   For *God hath spoke the word."*

From the preceding views she discerned clearly, that one more step must be taken ere she could fully test the faithfulness of God. "Faithful is he who hath called you, who also *will* do it," was now no longer a matter of opinion, but a truth confidently believed, and she saw that she must relinquish the confident expression before indulged in, as promising something in the *future,* "Thou wilt receive me," for the yet more confident expression, implying present assurance, "Thou *dost* receive!" It is, perhaps, almost needless to say, that the enemy who had heretofore endeavored to withstand every step of the Spirit's leadings, now confronted her, with much greater energy. The suggestion that it was strangely presumptuous to believe in such a way, was presented to her mind with a plausibility which only Satanic subtlety could invent. But the resolution to believe was fixed; and then the Spirit most inspiringly said to her heart, "The kingdom of heaven suffereth violence, and the violent take it by force."

And now, realizing that she was engaged in a transaction eternal in its consequences, she here, in the strength, and as in the presence of the Father, Son, and Holy Spirit, and those spirits that minister to the heirs of salvation, said, ""O, Lord, I call heaven and earth to witness that I *now lay body, soul, and spirit,* with *all these redeemed powers, upon thine altar, to be for ever* THINE! 'TIS DONE! Thou hast promised to receive me! Thou canst not be unfaithful! *Thou dost receive me now!* From this time henceforth I *am thine — wholly Thine!*"

The enemy suggested, "'Tis but the work of your own understanding — the effort of your own will." But the Spirit of the Lord raised up a standard which Satan, with his combined forces, could not overthrow. It was by the following presentation of truth that the Spirit helped her infirmities: "Do not your perceptions of right — even your *own understanding* — assure you that it is matter of *thanksgiving to God* that you have been thus enabled to present your all to him?" "Yes," responded her whole heart, "it has all been the work of the Spirit. I will praise him! Glory be to God in the highest! Worthy is the Lamb to receive glory, honor, and blessing! Hallelujah! the Lord God Omnipotent reigneth! Yes, thou dost reign unrivaled in my heart! Thou hast subdued all things to thyself, and now thou dost reign throughout the empire of my soul, the Lord God of every motion!" The SPIRIT now bore full testimony to her spirit, of the TRUTH of THE WORD! She felt in experimental verity that it was not in vain she had believed; her very existence seemed lost and swallowed up in God; she plunged, as it were, into an immeasurable ocean of love, light, and power, and realized that she was encompassed with the "favor of the Almighty as with a shield; and felt assured, while she continued thus, to rest her entire being on the faithfulness of God, she might confidently stand rejoicing in hope," and exultantly sing with the poet —

"My steadfast soul from falling free,
   Shall now no longer rove,
But Christ be all in all to me,
   And *all my soul be* LOVE."

She now saw infinite propriety, comprehensiveness, and beauty, in those words of DIVINE origin, from which she had before shrunk, as implying a state too high and sacred for ordinary attainment or expectation.

Holiness, Sanctification, *perfect love*, were words no longer so incomprehensible, or indefinite in nature or bearing, in relation to the individual experience of the Lord's redeemed ones. She wondered not that it should be said, in reference to the "WAY OF HOLINESS," "The *ransomed of the Lord shall walk there!*" She perceived that these terms were most significantly expressive of a state of soul in which every believer should live, and felt that no words of mere earthly origin could embody to her own perceptions, or convey to the understanding of others, half the comprehensiveness of meaning contained in them, and which stand forth so prominently in the word of God, thereby assuring men that they are given by the express dictation of the Holy Spirit.

She now thought of her former peculiar scruples in reference to the *use* of these words of divine origin, as in a degree partaking of the sin of Uzziah, implying, as she now clearly discerned, an unwarrantable carefulness about the ark of God; as though infinite wisdom had not devised the most proper mode of expression; for she well remembered how often her heart had risen against these expressions, as objectionable, when she had heard other travelers in the "way of holiness" use the terms as expressive of the state of grace into which the Lord had brought them; the very same words which she now saw were beautifully expressive of the state into which the Lord had brought her own soul.

But she now felt such a mighty increase of confidence in God, that she hesitated not to trust the entire management of his own cause in his own hands, and was willing, ay, even desirous, to become an instrument through which he might show forth his power to save unto the uttermost — to be accounted of no reputation — to be but as a "*voice*" to sound forth the praise of the "Almighty to save." She was willing that the instrument should be despised and rejected, so that the voice of God should alone be heard, and the Savior honored and accepted.

Chapter Seven

"They are not of the world, even as I am not of the world. I pray not that thou shouldest take them out of the world, but that thou shouldest keep them from the evil." - *The prayer of Jesus for his Disciples.*

"'Tis done! thou dost this moment save,
  With full salvation bless;
Redemption through thy blood I have,
  And spotless love and peace."

Now that she was so powerfully and experimentally assured of the blessedness of this "shorter way," O, with what ardor of soul did she long to say to every redeemed one, "Ye have been fully redeemed; redeemed from all iniquity, that ye should be unto God a peculiar people, zealous of good works!"

So reasonable did it appear, that *all the Lord's ransomed ones,* who had been so fully redeemed, and *chosen out of the world,* should be *sanctified,* set apart for holy service, as chosen vessels unto God, to bear his hallowed name before a gainsaying world, by having the seal legibly enstamped upon the forehead, proclaiming them as "not of the world," a "peculiar people to show forth his praise;" that all the energies of her mind were now absorbed in the desire to communicate the living intensity of her soul on this subject to the heart of every professed disciple.

Her now newly-inspired spirit could scarcely conceive of a higher ambition, in the present state of existence, than to be endued with the unction of the Holy One, and then permitted, by the power of the Spirit, to say to every lover of Jesus, "This is the will of God, even your sanctification;" Jesus, *your* Redeemer, your Savior, waits even now to sanctify you wholly; "and I pray God that your *whole spirit,* and *soul,* and *body,* be preserved blameless unto the coming of our Lord Jesus Christ. Faithful is he that calleth you, who also will do it."

It was in that same hallowed hour when she was first, through the blood of the everlasting covenant, permitted to enter within the veil, and prove the blessedness of the "way of holiness," that the weighty responsibilities, and also inconceivably-glorious destination of the believer, were unfolded to her spiritual vision, in a manner inexpressibly surpassing her former perceptions.

She seemed permitted to look down through the vista of the future, to behold herself as having begun a race, in a way luminously lit up by the rays of the Sun of righteousness, with the gaze of myriads of interested spectators — ay, even the gaze of the upper, as also the lower, world — intensely fixed upon her, watching her progress in a course that seemed to admit of no respite, or turning to the right or to the left, and where consequences, inconceivably momentous, and eternal in duration, were pending.

Have you brought yourself into this state of blessedness? Is it through your own exertions that this light has been kindled in your heart? were the inquiries which were now urged upon her attention. She deeply felt, as her heart responded to these interrogatories, that it was all the work of the Spirit; and never before did such a piercing sense of her own demerit and helplessness penetrate her mind as at that hour, while her inmost soul replied, 'Tis from the "Father of lights," the "Giver of every good and perfect gift," that I have received this precious *gift.* Yes, it is a *gift* from God, and to his name be all the glory!

The Spirit then suggested, *If* it is a *gift from God,* God is not exclusive in the impartation of his gifts and you will be required to declare it; to declare it as his gift, through our Lord Jesus Christ, ready for the acceptance of all, as his free gift; and this, if you would retain the blessing, will not be left to your own choice. You will be called to profess this blessing before thousands! Can you do it? And here she was permitted again to count the cost. She had been saying, Rather let me die than lose the blessing, for Satan had suggested that she would ever be vacillating in her experience; one day professing the blessing, and another not; that she was so constitutionally prone to reason, it would require an extraordinary miracle to sustain her amid the array of unpropitious circumstances, which, like a mighty phalanx, crowded before the vision of her mind: but the Spirit brought to her remembrance. the continuous miracle of the Israelitish nation, fed daily with bread directly from heaven. And though assured that a miracle equal in magnitude would be constantly requisite for her support, yet she gloried in the assurance that the same almighty power stood continuously pledged for its performance. And now that she was called to count the cost of coming out in the profession of this blessing before thousands, the enemy directed her mind most powerfully to what her former failures had been, in reference to making confession with the mouth.

In few duties had she more frequently brought condemnation on her soul than in this; and the suggestion from the adversary, that a failure in this requirement was precisely the ground on which she should lose the blessing, assumed more plausibility than former temptations. But the Spirit raised up a standard; and she was enabled to resolve to be a. worker together with God, in such a manner, that the onward pilgrimage of more than five succeeding years has tested the happy consequences of the decision, and proved that it was indeed the Spirit of the Lord that raised the standard — the Spirit that taught!

The matter was decided thus: Some settled principles must be established in the soul, by which it may be known what shall constitute duty in reference to this subject. Duty must be determined by a reference to the requirements of the Word; and being settled thus, the voice of duty is literally the *voice of God to the soul*. She was then enabled to decide the matter of testifying to the work of the Spirit thus: The church is represented as Christ's body. I am one of the members of that body. If I, by testifying of the Spirit's operation on my heart, am individually benefited, the whole body is advantaged, by a more healthy action being produced throughout, while if I neglect to testify, and, in consequence, suffer loss, my relation to the body will of necessity cause it to participate in that loss. It is plain, therefore, and beyond all contradiction, my duty to declare the work of God. The health of my own soul and that of the precious body of Christ, of which I am a member, demand its performance

The inquiry then arose, But am I by my own power of reasoning to determine in matters so momentous? The answer was, If you have power to reason above an idiot, or the beasts that perish, God has given that power; it is a talent intrusted, for which you will be called to render an account of stewardship. *Natural* abilities are as truly *gifts from God* as those termed by men *gracious* abilities. Grace does not render natural endowments in any degree useless, it only turns them into a *sanctified* channel.

Having received, through these gracious communications, more enlightened and confirmed views of duty, and feeling assured that the voice of duty was in verity the voice of God she was enabled to resolve that however formidable the circumstances were, if it literally cost life in the effort to go forward, she would still proceed; and though a martyr to the cause, it should be enough that the Almighty had said, "Go forward." On coming to this point, a yet more glorious increase of light burst upon her way! The Spirit brought to her remembrance the words she had most solemnly uttered but a few moments before, when, making the sacred dedication of all her powers for ever to God, she had used the dedicatory words of David, "Into thy hands I commit my spirit, for thou hast redeemed me, O Lord God of truth." She had *realized* and acknowledged the offering accepted. And now the Spirit said, Had your spirit actually left the body, and mingled with the spirits before the throne, when you thus solemnly committed it into the hands of God; and had the Father of spirits permitted you to return and again actuate that body, for the special purpose of declaring before thousands that Jesus is a full Savior, able to save to the uttermost, could you do it?

She thought of the blood-washed spirits surrounding in waiting attitude the eternal throne, and, from a newly-received affinity of feeling, began to conjecture their burning ardor, as messengers of love, to communicate tidings of grace to whatever sphere commissioned. She thought of one sent to the earth with a special embassy charged to communicate it to the greatest possible number of its inhabitants; she conjectured the zeal he would manifest in giving publicity to the tidings, the expedients he would use, the ideas of his auditors relative to the importance of his mission, their probable indifference, perhaps contumely and scorn, pronouncing him over-zealous, charging him with carrying matters too far — perchance fanatic, or monomaniac might be the epithets that would serve to distinguish him from the mass of mankind, and be the reward of his labors of love, during the performance of his earthly mission.

Yet the thought of the manner in which these considerations would affect him, the various motives that would call forth his commiseration, the little weight which a contemptuous reception of his message would have on his personal feelings, only so far as the honor of his Sovereign was concerned, his slight associations and attachments to earth, except as the place for the completion of his work, his thoughts of heaven, as the end of his operations, the *home* of his heart, his *native* country, &c., all tended to instruct and admonish her.

It was now that the Scriptural meaning of the words, "The very God of peace sanctify you wholly," "body, soul and spirit," "thy will be done on earth as it is done in heaven," "ye are not of the world, I have chosen you out of the world," "redeemed from all iniquity," a *peculiar* people," "strangers," "pilgrims," with the saints in light," &c., poured torrent after torrent of light upon the peculiar nature, responsibilities, and infinite blessedness of the way upon which she had newly entered. And in answer to the inquiry, Can you declare this great salvation to others? her heart responded, Yea, Lord, to an assembled world at once, if it be at thy bidding! Only "arm me with thy Spirit's might." "Into thy hands I commit my spirit;" let it but actuate this body for the performance of thy good will and pleasure in all things: and if at any time thou seest me about to depart from thee, cut short the work in righteousness and take me home to thyself.

"'Tis done! the great transaction's done,
    I am my Lord's, and he is mine;
He drew me, and I follow'd on,
    Charm'd to confess the voice divine.
Now rest, my long-divided heart,
    Fix'd on this blissful center rest,
Nor ever from thy Lord depart,
    With him of every good possess'd."

Chapter Eight - There Is But One Way

"Sanctify them through thy truth: thy word is truth."

Light from the eternal hills!
    Thou lamp of life divine!
River of God, of many rills,
    Reaching to all mankind.

Laden with precious freight,
    Fresh from the courts above,
Alike to all, both small and great,
    Thine embassy of love.

Gold were a thing of naught,
    Rubies of priceless worth,
Compared with treasures thou hast brought
    To fallen sons of earth.

O how precious, precious beyond all computation was the blessed word of God now to her soul! She had valued it before; but now, as she retraced the way by which the Lord had brought her, she saw that each progressive step had been distinctly marked by a reference to its requirements.

Though often greatly advantaged by the recital of the experience of fellow-travelers to the heavenly city, so much so that she greatly loved the assembling of themselves together, yet she found, on looking back, that former perplexities in experience had too frequently arisen from a proneness to follow the traditions of men, instead of the oracles of God.

She now found that *"there is but one way,"* and this way far better, and *"shorter,"* also, by bringing every diversified state of experience, however specious or complex, to compare with the "law and the testimony." And if not according to these, she became assured it was because the true light had not been followed. From this period, therefore, it became an immovable axiom with her, never to deem an experience satisfactory that could not be substantiated with an emphatic, *"Thus saith the Lord."*

On getting into "the way of holiness," she found much clearer light beaming upon her path. Never in former experience did she so sweetly apprehend the truth of the words, "Thy sun shall no more go down, neither shall thy moon withdraw itself: for the Lord shall be thy everlasting light." "And the days of thy mourning shall be ended."

It was while walking in this light that the subtlety, maliciousness, and power of the arch deceiver became much more apparent, and would have become a matter of much more dread, were it not that by the same light she also discovered, with the prophet's servant, when his eyes were opened, that more were they that were for her, than all that were against her. And then the knowledge that she was, in experimental verity, *resting upon Christ,* the anointed of God, imparted such an increase of holy energy, realizing, as she did momentarily, that virtue came out of Jesus, her Savior and Redeemer, for the full supply of all her wants, under every variety of circumstance, that she was indeed enabled to obey the command, "Rejoice evermore." And then she became so divinely assured also that the "trial of her faith, was *precious*," that it was not hard to "glory in tribulation."

Her perceptions of the absolute need of the atonement were never so vivid as while journeying onward in this way. She felt she could not take one progressive step, or for one moment present an acceptable sacrifice, but through the merits of her Savior. Yet though so deeply realizing the truth of her Savior's words, *"Without me ye can do nothing,"* she felt also it would not be to the honor of his great name, should she not live in the enjoyment of that state of salvation, in which she should be enabled to say, *"I can do all things through Christ which strengtheneth me."*

In reference to temptation, she learned from experience that "the disciple is not above his Master." She ever found that trials, well circumstanced in fiendish subtlety, beset her way. But by the increase of light which beamed upon her path as she entered the highway of holiness, she could now, with much stronger confidence, exclaim, "We are not ignorant of his devices." The remembrance was sweetly encouraging to her soul, that the Savior was in all points tempted like as we are, yet *without sin* — and to know she had the same weapons to contend with that the blessed Savior used when on earth, the same potent sword of the Spirit, was the rejoicing of her heart.

Yet she did not find the "highway of holiness" a place for inglorious ease, but that it was indeed, as significantly implied in the Scriptural phrase, "A WAY," requiring, to her mind, by the peculiar construction of the expression, *interminable progression!*

And yet she loved to call it the "rest of faith," and joyously, as illustrative of her experience, said with the apostle, "For we which have believed *do* enter into rest." Yet she could not conceive of a rest sweeter to the follower of Jesus than to *do the will of God*.

The standard for Christian imitation she deemed to be established by inspiration — "Let that mind be in you that was in Christ;" and the most conclusive way of coming to the knowledge of duty, a reference to the Spirit and example of Christ. In conformity with these principles, it was not surprising that she should regard that state of soul which would constrain the disciple of Jesus to say, "The zeal of thine house hath eaten me up," as in any degree incompatible with the assurance of having entered into this state of rest; but regarded the proportion in which this conformity to Christ was realized, the amount of evidence of having entered into the *rest of faith* – "the way of holiness."

The standard of Christian excellence being thus fixed by the ratio of approximation to the image of Christ, wherever she saw the characteristics of his loveliness most clearly described, the more abundant was her love.

She well knew that in the present imperfect state of existence, where we necessarily know but in part, and where perfection can only exist in the gospel sense, which ordains that "love be the fulfilling of the law," there is need for the constant exercise of that "charity that suffereth long, and is kind;" and wherever she saw this spirit most sweetly exemplified by corresponding action, there was her heart most enduringly united; and though she was most endearingly attached to the division of Christ's body where from infancy she had been graciously cherished, yet the point of attraction was centered in the nearest resemblance to the image of the Savior; and where the most uniform exhibition of the mind that was in Christ, inducing conformity to his will, was recognized, her heart with most endearing emotion exclaimed, "The same is my brother, my sister, my mother!"

It was thus, from what she deemed the requirement and spirit of the blessed Bible, that a foundation was laid for a characteristic in her experience which was a source of much satisfaction to herself and others; and she wondered not that one of blessed memory, while walking in this "highway," should exclaim, Here

"Names, and sects and parties fall,
And Christ alone is all in all"

Chapter Nine

"Having, therefore, brethren, boldness to enter into the holiest by the blood of Jesus by a new and living way, which he hath consecrated for us through the veil, that is to say, his flesh, and having a high priest over the house of God, let us draw nigh with a true heart, in full assurance of faith, having our bodies sprinkled from an evil conscience, and our bodies washed with pure water." - *New Testament.*

It may be asked, And how did the process described in the preceding numbers eventuate in that disciple being brought into the holiest by the blood of Jesus? Did the resolution to be a Bible Christian — the determination to consecrate all to God by laying all upon the altar of sacrifice — or the act of entering into the bonds of an everlasting covenant to be wholly the Lord's — bring about this entrance into the new and living way? How could these purposes, however well intentioned, result in having the heart sprinkled from an evil conscience, and the body washed with pure water? Can aught but the blood of Christ do this?

Perhaps few with more conscious poverty of spirit would respond in the negative to these inquiries, than that traveler in the king's highway, whose experience has been alluded to.

"Jesus, my Lord, thy blood alone
Hath power sufficient to atone,"

were the confirmed sentiments of her heart. "Not by works of righteousness which we have done, but according to his mercy he saveth us; by the washing of regeneration and renewing of the Holy Ghost," was the response ever uppermost in her heart in answer to such inquiries. Yet she conceived that it was by these pious resolves she was enabled thus to be a worker together with God. God cannot be unfaithful, rested with weight upon her mind as an absorbing truth; and some principles founded on the faithfulness of God, by the testing of which she became assured that "it is a good thing that the heart be established in grace,' were as follows:-

God, in his infinite love, has provided a way by which lost, guilty men may be redeemed, justified, cleansed, and saved, with the power of an endless life. Provision has thus been made for the restoration of man, by availing himself of which, in the way designated in the Scriptures, he may regain that which was lost in Adam — even the image of God re-enstamped upon the soul.

To bring about this restoration, the Father so loved the world that he gave his only-begotten Son, who from eternity had dwelt in his bosom. At the appointed time, Christ, the anointed of God, was revealed, and, as our example, lived a life of disinterested devotion to the interests of mankind; and, as the Lamb slain from the foundation of the world, laid himself upon the altar; "tasted death for every man," and "bore the sins of the whole world in his own body." As an assurance of the amplitude of his grace, and that he is no respecter of persons, he hath said, "And I, if I be lifted up, will draw all men unto me." "The Spirit of truth which proceedeth from the Father, he shall testify of me." The Spirit, true to its appointed office, reproves of sin, righteousness, and judgment. And now the entire voice of divine revelation proclaims "*all* things ready!" The Spirit and the Bride say, Come!

The altar, thus provided by the conjoint testimony of the Father, Son, and Holy Spirit, is Christ. His sacrificial death and sufferings are the sinner's plea; the immutable promises of the Lord Jehovah the ground of claim. If true to the Spirit's operations on the heart, men, as workers together with God, confess their sins, the faithfulness and justice of God stand pledged not only to *forgive,* but also to *cleanse from all unrighteousness.*

By the resolve to be a "Bible Christian," this traveler in the "way of holiness" placed herself in the way to receive the direct teachings of the Spirit, and in the one and the only way for the attainment of the salvation promised in the gospel of Christ, inasmuch as it is written, "He became the author of eternal salvation to all them that *obey him.*"

And by the determination to consecrate all upon the altar of sacrifice to God, with the resolve to "enter into the bonds of an everlasting covenant to be wholly the Lord's for time and eternity," and then acting in conformity with this decision, *actually laying all upon the altar,* by the most unequivocal Scripture testimony, she laid herself under the most solemn obligation to *believe that the sacrifice became the Lord's property; and by virtue of the altar upon which the offering was laid, became "holy" and" acceptable."*

The written testimony of the Old and New Testament Scriptures upon which, to her mind, the *obligation* for this belief rested, was brought out by comparing the design and bearing of the old and new covenant dispensations, thus — The old ordained that an altar be erected. See Exod. xxvii, 1, &c. This altar, before being eligible for the reception of offerings, was to be "atoned for," cleansed, and sanctified. See Exod. xxix, 36, 37. This being done, it was ordained by God to be "an altar most holy; whatsoever toucheth the altar shall be holy.' Being thus proclaimed by the fiat of the Holy One "an altar *most holy,*" whatever *touched* the altar became holy, virtually the *Lord's property, sanctified to his service.* The sacredness and perpetuity of this ordinance were recognized by God manifest in the flesh," centuries afterward. "The *altar* that sanctifieth the gift." See Matt. xxiii, 19.

As the old dispensation but shadowed forth good things to come, so under the new Christ is apprehended as the bringer in of a better hope. "For their sakes I *sanctify* myself, that they also may be *sanctified* through the truth," said the blessed Savior, in praying for his disciples. "Neither pray I for *these* alone, but for them also which shall *believe on me* through their word." Here she beheld the *Christian altar,* so exultingly recognized by the apostle to the Hebrews, in contradistinction to the Jewish altar: Heb. xiii, 10, "We have an altar, whereof they have no right to eat which serve the tabernacle. Wherefore Jesus also, that he might sanctify the people with his own blood, suffered without the gate. Let us go forth therefore unto him," &c. He taketh away the first, that he may establish the *second!* And here she beheld an "altar most holy." If; under the old covenant, it was ordained," "Whatsoever toucheth the altar shall be holy," her heart, in its confident exultations, said, "How much more shall the blood of Christ, who, through the eternal Spirit, offered himself without spot to God, purge your conscience from dead works to serve the living God !" Here she beheld the Lamb of God that taketh away the sins of the world!

It was thus, by "laying all upon this altar," she, by the most unequivocal Scripture testimony, laid herself under the most sacred obligation to *believe* that the sacrifice became "holy and acceptable," and virtually the *Lord's property,* even by virtue of the sanctity of the *altar* upon which it was laid, and continued "holy and acceptable," so long as kept inviolably upon this hallowed altar. At an early stage of her experience in the "way of holiness," the Holy Spirit powerfully opened to her understanding the following passage, as corroborative of this view of the subject: Rom. xii, 1, "I beseech you therefore, brethren, by the mercies of God, that ye present your bodies a living sacrifice, holy, acceptable unto God, which is your reasonable service."

From these important considerations she perceived that it was indeed by the Spirit's teachings she had been led to "enter into the bonds of an everlasting covenant to be wholly the Lord's," inasmuch as by the removal of this offering from off this *hallowing* altar, she should *cease to be holy,* as it is "the altar that sanctifieth the gift." In this light she also saw why it is, that all is so imperatively required, inasmuch as it is the Redeemer who makes the demand for the "living sacrifice," having purchased all, body, soul, and spirit, unto himself. And she wondered not that an offering *consciously* not entire — known by the offerer to be less than *all* — is not acceptable, inasmuch as God has pronounced such offerings unacceptable. See Malachi i, 8, 13, 14. And that such an offering is not received, even though the reception of it be greatly desired by the offerer, she thought to be scripturally accounted for by the same prophet, ii, 13. And that such a one could not believe while still halting between the world and an *entire surrender,* she thought fully explained by the words of the Savior, "How can ye believe who receive honor one of another, and seek not that honor which cometh from God only?" And this she believed to be the hindrance with thousands of professed disciples who hear the sayings of Jesus, and desire holiness, and yet, by refusing to come to his terms, affirm that his sayings are hard; while many go back altogether, and follow the Savior no more! notwithstanding he so confidently and persuasively affirms, "If any man *will do* his will he shall *know* of the doctrine."

It was on coming to *this altar* she was enabled to realize *how* it is that the devotions of the believer, while resting here, are "unto God a sweet savor of Christ," inasmuch as no service can be "holy, acceptable" unto God, unless presented through this medium.

The duty of believing, and also of having a *Scriptural* foundation for faith to rest upon, she regarded as most important, and feeling assured that God has so explicitly given, in his written word, a thorough foundation for our faith, she saw the sin of unbelief so *dishonoring to God,* that she wondered not the "fearful and unbelieving" should be excluded from the believer's rest, and numbered by the Revelator in such revolting companionship.

And thus, as has been related, she found the "*shorter,* the *one,* and the *only way,*" of which it is said, "The redeemed of the Lord shall walk there," by surrendering all to the Redeemer, and venturing, *believingly,* the entire being upon *Jesus!* Resting here, she proved, experimentally, the truth of his declaration, "I am the way," and was enabled to realize continually the purifying virtue of his atoning blood, and to testify that it was not in vain he had "offered himself up that he might sanctify the people with his own blood."

And though she apprehended that nothing *but the blood of Jesus* could *sanctify* and *cleanse* from sin, yet she was also scripturally assured that it was needful for the recipient of this grace, as a worker together with God, to place himself believingly *upon* "the altar that sanctifieth the gift;" ere he could prove the efficacy of the all-cleansing blood. Gracious intentions, and strong desires, she was convinced, are not sufficient to bring about these important results; corresponding action is also necessary; the offering must be *brought* and believingly *laid upon the altar,* ere the acceptance of it can be realized. In this crucifixion of nature, the Spirit helpeth our infirmities, and worketh mightily to *will* — but *man must act.*

As illustrative, in a degree, of her views of responsibility, she would refer to a would-be offerer at the Jewish altar, for months graciously intending to present the sacrifices required by the law, yet deferring, from a variety of causes, seemingly plausible, to *comply* with the requirement by handing over his gift, until the law, which he had ever acknowledged "just and good," cuts him off from the community of his people. And thus she was apprehensive that many who graciously intend to be holy, by laying all upon the Christian altar, from various seemingly-plausible causes, are delaying to *comply* with the requirement, "Be ye holy," until, at an unlooked-for hour, the law, which they have ever pronounced "just and good," excludes them from the community of the redeemed, blood-washed company in heaven.

She also found one act of faith not sufficient to insure a continuance in the "way of holiness," but that a *continuous* act was requisite. "As ye have received Christ Jesus the Lord, so walk ye in him," was an admonition greatly blessed to her soul. Assured that there was no other way of retaining this state of grace but by the exercise of the same resoluteness of character, presenting *all* and *keeping* all upon the hallowed altar, and also in the exercise of the same faith, she was enabled, through the teachings of the Spirit, "to walk by the same rule, and mind the same thing," and for years continued an onward walk in the "way of holiness."

Being thus impelled by a divine constraint to test every progressive step by the powerful persuasive, "Thus it is written," she became increasingly confident in her rejoicings, "that her faith did not stand in the wisdom of men, but in the power of God;" and instead of being "vacillating in her experience," as had been so painfully suggested by the tempter, she was enabled daily to become more firmly rooted and grounded in the faith, abounding therein with thanksgiving.

It was thus that, through the Spirit's teachings, she was ready to give an answer to those that asked a reason of her hope, and these teachings were communicated most peculiarly through the medium of the *written word*. *Through* each succeeding year of her pilgrimage in the heavenly way she learned to place a yet higher estimate upon its truths. The nearer she drew to the city of her God, the clearer was the light that shone upon its sacred pages, proclaiming it to be the WORD OF THE LORD; and as she continued to pass down through time, leaning on its sacred declarations, she verily believed herself to be as divinely sustained as though to her *outward perceptions* she knew and could *feel* herself leaning for support upon the "FAITHFUL" and "TRUE," "with vesture dipped in blood," called, by the Revelator, the "WORD or GOD!"

"Thy statutes have been my song in the house of my pilgrimage." — David.

Blessed Bible! how I love it!
   How it doth my bosom cheer:
What hath earth like this to covet?
   O, what stores of wealth are here!
Man was lost, and doom'd to sorrow,
   Not one ray of light or bliss
Could he from earth's treasures borrow,
   Till his way was cheer'd by this.

Yes, I'll to my bosom press thee,
   PRECIOUS WORD, I'll hide thee here;
Sure my very heart will bless thee,
   For thou ever sayest, "Good cheer!"
Speak, my heart, and tell thy ponderings,
   Tell how far thy rovings led, When
THIS BOOK brought back thy wanderings,
   Speaking life as from the dead.

Yes, sweet Bible! I will hide thee
   Deep, yes, *deeper* in this heart;
Thou, through all my life wilt guide me,
   And in death we will not part.
Part in death? No! never! never!
   Through death's vale I'll lean on thee;
Then, in worlds above, for ever,
   Sweeter still thy truths shall be!

Notes by the Way

Chapter One

"Gather up the fragments, that nothing be lost." — The Savior.

"And thou shalt remember all the way which the Lord thy God led thee these forty years in the wilderness, to humble thee and to prove thee, to know what was in thy heart, whether thou wouldst keep his commandments or no. And he humbled thee, and suffered thee to hunger, and fed thee with manna which thou knewest not, neither did thy fathers know; that he might make thee know that man doth not live by bread only, but by every word that proceedeth out of the mouth of the Lord doth man live." — *Deut.* viii, 2, 3.

On reviewing the entire way by which the Lord had brought her onward through the pilgrimage of life, she saw the faithfulness of God exhibited throughout, in manner calculated permanently to assure her heart that with him there is, in truth, "no variableness, neither shadow of turning." At the dawn of life she had been intrusted to parents to whom the Father of spirits had said, "Take this child and bring it up for me." They felt the solemn responsibility, and endeavored to train her up for God.

God did not forget to encourage their efforts. He watered the seed sown with the dews of grace from her earliest recollections. When not four years old, powerful conviction for sin gave assurance that the Holy Spirit was true to the performance of its promised aid.

Though for many happy years she was enabled to testify, with perfect assurance, that she had passed from death unto life, yet the precise time when that change took place she could never state. Not to have an experience like most others born into the kingdom of Christ, who are so fully able, from the overwhelming circumstances of the occasion, to state the precise moment, was a fruitful source of temptation, resulting in years of painful solicitate.

From a child it was her error to treasure up, in careful remembrance, those outward exhibitions, which are given by many sincere disciples, of the inward workings of the Spirit. Hence she was too often led to pronounce upon the magnitude of the work wrought in the heart, by the outward manifestations of feeling.

Not infrequently she felt like weeping because she could not weep, imagining if she could plunge herself into those overwhelming sorrows, and despairing views of relationship to God, spoken of by some, she could then come and throw herself upon his mercy with greater probability of success.

Over and again, after having had a long season in wrestling with God, she would, as a last resource, say, "If thou wilt but direct me by thy word, and permit me to open to some passage suited to my case, I will, through thy grace assisting me, abide by its decisions. And at several never-to-be-forgotten periods did the Lord condescend to give the most direct answers of peace in this manner. For a time she would rejoice in the consolation received, and glory in the assurances of the blessed word as in verity the voice of God to her soul; but as soon as the freshness of these visitations passed over, she would again give way to dissatisfaction with her experience.

This dissatisfaction did not generally arise from the consideration that her experience was unscriptural, but from the fact that it was so unlike what she conceived to be the manner of the Spirit's operation on the hearts of others, who, as she conjectured, had received the assurance of acceptance in some such luminous manner, independent, in part, from Scriptural demonstration, that they had been constrained *irresistibly* to believe.

Uncertainty and spiritual depression were the consequences resulting from these repeated turnings away from the word of the Lord to the feeble testimony of men. And it is not surprising while this course, which was so dishonoring to God, was, in any degree, persisted in, that she should be left to comparative desertion. Yet this was for years her course.

Sometimes, during this period, the adversary tried to urge upon her mind that the ways of the Lord were unequal; intimating that he bestowed a much larger share of spiritual illumination on some than on others, when the true state of the case was, that she was possessed of the spirit of a Naaman, or of the unbelieving Jews — resolved that, unless she should see *signs* and *wonders,* she would not believe.

On reviewing this portion of her experience, she afterward saw that the ways of God could not have been justified, in imparting any other state of experience than that of uncertainty and spiritual depression, inasmuch as he hath said, "If ye will not believe, surely ye shall not be established." Yet, notwithstanding all this waywardness, she greatly desired God as the portion. of her soul, and often felt as if she could say, that his favor was more desirable than life. With deep groaning of spirit, her heart gave utterance to its emotions in saying, —

"Let me no more, in deep Complaint,
   'My leanness! O, my leanness!" cry;
Alone consumed with pining want,
   Of all my Father's children I."

"Believe — only believe," was the oft-repeated admonition of the friends of Jesus; and her heart would as frequently silently ejaculate, "But *what* and *how* am I to believe?" till she became nearly wearied with what seemed to her an almost unmeaning admonition, unaccompanied, as it most generally was, with the necessary explanations.

When about thirteen she acknowledged herself, before the world, as a seeker of salvation, and united herself with the people of God. One night, about this time, after having wrestled with the Lord till about midnight, she sought the repose of her pillow with feelings expressed by the poet —

"I'll weary thee with my complaint,
   Here, at thy feet, for ever lie,
With longing sick, with groaning faint –
   O! give me love, or else I die."

She believed herself to have fallen asleep, when, with a power that aroused body and mind by its heavenly sweetness, these words were spoken to her inmost soul, —

"See Israel's gentle Shepherd stands,
   With all-engaging charms;
See how he calls the tender lambs,
   And folds them in his arms."

The place seemed to shine with the glory of God; and she felt that the blessed Savior indeed took her to the bosom of his love, and bade her "be of good cheer." All was light, joy, and peace.

She had no recollection of ever having heard those sweet lines before, and regarded them as spoken directly from the lips of the good Shepherd to her heart; but on observing them some years afterward in a sabbath-school hymn book, she conjectured that the words might have been seed sown in her infant heart at a very early age, when cherished in one of these nurseries of the Lord.

The consolation at this time derived was of several days' duration, but she again yielded to her former unwise course, and began to measure herself by the standard of experience established by others, instead of going to the law and the testimony, as enjoined by the word; and it would, as before observed, have been inconsistent with the declarations of that word for her to enjoy an established state of experience, while indulging in such a course. Had she taken "the sword of the Spirit," it would have guarded the way of life and happiness, and have prevented this waywardness, by presenting the admonitory sentence of an inspired apostle, "For we dare not make ourselves of the number, or compare ourselves with some that commend themselves, but they measuring themselves by themselves, and comparing themselves among themselves, are not wise." See 2 Cor. x, 12.

Had she only taken the word of the Lord as closely to the companionship of her heart during this part of her pilgrimage, as she did in the, pathway of after years, when she sought unto it, as the man of her counsel, under all circumstances of difficulty, she would have found

"Here light descending from above
   Directs the doubtful feet –
Here promises of heavenly love

>   Our ardent wishes meet.
> Our num'rous wants are here redrest,
>   And all our wants supplied;
> Naught we can ask to make us blest
>   Is in THIS BOOK denied."

Chapter Two

>   O'er life's rough ocean wave
>   Fast was I going,
> By threat'ning tempests driven, and billow tost,
>   And surges deep of wo
>   My soul o'erflowing!
> O, all seem'd lost without thee -- lost, all lost.
>
>   My star of earthly bliss
>   Set in deep sorrow –
> One glimpse from thee had all its lustre cost,
>   And not one gleam of light
>   Could it e'er borrow,
> For in thy lucent beams it all was lost -- all lost.

At another time, about a year subsequent to the period just alluded to, the Lord again greatly comforted her soul during the night season. She had again, as on the former occasion, been for a long time wrestling earnestly with God, till nature had become wearied; when, on falling asleep, she dreamed she was standing without. The canopy of a beautiful midnight sky was spread out above her; the firmament was cloudless, and the full moon was silently walking the heavens. A stillness, that seemed hallowed to something unusual, reigned, but her eye was intently fixed, and her mind all absorbed by the attraction of a bright star. Presently it began to enlarge its circle, wider and yet wider, when (as she continued to keep her eye fixed on the point where it first began to rest) the form of the infant Savior was presented, and these words were proclaimed, "For unto us a child is born, unto us a son is given. And his name shall be called WONDERFUL, COUNSELOR, THE MIGHTY GOD, THE EVERLASTING FATHER, THE PRINCE OF PEACE."

In the mean time, while these words were being proclaimed, the circle rapidly widened, until the whole heavens had become encircled in one glow of glory.

The happy experience of succeeding years, when, by keeping her eye steadily fixed upon the Day-star from on high, her spiritual horizon had become enlightened, and, as she had continued to gaze, had rapidly taken in yet wider and still wider circles of glory, until the whole firmament of her soul had become radiant with its blissful beams, assured her that this communication was intended to convey a greater infinitude of meaning than her feeble capacities comprehended at the time.

It was not until she had received Jesus as her full Savior, and her spiritual heavens had been lighted up by the revelation of Christ to her soul as the Wonderful, Counselor, The mighty God, The everlasting Father, The Prince of Peace, that she was enabled to have anything like proper perceptions of the infinite condescension of God in this communication. It was then she exultantly sung —

> My faith hath caught the gaze,
> I now behold thee;
> And now let tempests wing their chilling frost,
> Thy mildly-melting ray
> Beams sweetly o'er me –
> But without thee I am lost - in darkness lost
>
> O, yes, thou hast arisen
> In beauteous splendor,
> Thy radiance pure still rests my path across,
> And homage at thy shrine
> I'll ever render,
> Till in thy light I'm lost - for ever lost.

Though this was in a measure blest soul, at the time when given, and tended to assure her heart more confidently of the gracious designs of Infinite Love toward her, yet the impression soon passed away, and she relapsed into her former habits of reasoning and unbelief.

Chapter Three

"Come and let us reason together." — *The Word of the Lord*.

Being naturally much given to reasoning, seldom disposed to credit an assertion without an ostensible wherefore, she sometimes almost yielded to the suggestion, that her constitutional temperament was so greatly to her disadvantage, she need scarcely expect to be strong in faith —imagining that persons naturally credulous had in spiritual matters greatly the advantage of those who required a specified reason for every item of belief, and who most cautiously examined step by step the validity of the ground, ere the venture was made to tread firmly.

Yet this very trait of character, which she had habituated herself to regard as so unpropitious, when brought into obedience to Christ, was made subservient to her spiritual advantage.

She afterward found that God did not require her to believe anything but what was thoroughly substantiated by the requirements of his written word; and became convinced that it was not only her privilege, but also made her duty by the express declarations of that word, to test every step as she passed onward in the heavenly way, by a careful *searching of the Scriptures, in order to prove the validity of each step as successively taken.*

This course she afterward found to be necessary, not only for the establishment of her own soul, in order to its being rooted and grounded, so as not to be easily moved away from the hope of the gospel, but also as a prerequisite, not to be dispensed with, if she would honor God by being able to give an answer, with meekness and fear, to those who asked a reason of her hope.

But she lost beyond all calculation by thus lingering for years in this comparatively-undecided course. Some estimation of the irreparable loss sustained may be conceived by an allusion to one who in a given time is required to build an edifice. He lays the foundation, and begins to advance with the superstructure, but, fearful of some mistake, he overthrows it, and then again commences, and after having made, perchance, still higher advances, again demolishes it from the fear that something may yet be wrong. And this was precisely her unwise course.

It was not until she was enabled, through grace, to resolve on ceasing to have her mind influenced in its decisions by a reference to the experience of others, and determined, with a resoluteness not to be shaken, to take the BIBLE as her COUNSELOR, that she was enabled to make much progress in the divine life. But when she came to this decision, the Spirit began mightily to help her infirmities.

The hour will never be forgotten when, with a settled purpose of soul, she looked abroad on every motive of earthly ambition, and deliberately counted all things loss for the excellency of the knowledge of Jesus Christ; it was then that the Spirit said encouragingly, and also assuringly, "A door great and effectual is opened but there are many adversaries."

From that moment she became more understandingly convinced than ever, that there were foes for her to face, and more truly aware of the significant import of the inquiries

"Must I be carried to the skies
   On flowery beds of ease,
While others fought to win the prize,
   And sail'd through bloody seas?

"Are there no foes for me to face?
   Must I not stem the flood?
Is this vile world a friend to grace,
   To help me on to God?"

Chapter Four

"And one of the elders answered, saying unto me, Who are these which are arrayed in white robes? and whence came they? And I said unto him, Thou knowest. And he said unto me, These are they which came out of great tribulation, and have washed their robes and made them white in the blood of the Lamb." - *St. John.*

From this time she became assured, that *no less devotion* of spirit is required to carry the follower of Jesus unpolluted through this present evil world, than that which bore the martyrs through the flames. And she wondered not that it should be said in reply to the inquiries relative to the blood-washed company before the throne, "These are they which came out of great tribulation."

She then thought of the observation of the wise man, "The diligent hand maketh rich." Also of the student who trims the midnight lamp, in order to be learned in mere earthly science; and resolved that every consideration should be subservient to this one prominent motive of ambition, viz., to be well skilled in the science of holy living: judging that if the child of mortality would thus rise early and sit up late, and eat the bread of carefulness, as is not infrequently the case, in order to accumulate earthly knowledge, and often with no higher aim than earthly distinction, much more should the child of immortality, who has commenced an ever-enduring existence, by careful diligence, and patient, prayerful investigation, study to show himself approved in the sight of God and man, by having the deathless spirit well skilled in the science of immortality. From that time the intimations of the Spirit encouragingly assured her that this spiritual culture would not only tell on the pages of time, but would also speak on the records of eternity. And the infinite propriety of preparing the soul for an entrance into the abode of immortality became most apparent. And the literature of the Bible she believed to be the literature of heaven.

It was with the importance of these sentiments deeply written upon her heart that she began to imitate the example of the Savior, and rise while the world around her were yet slumbering, in order to commune with God, to *"search the Scriptures,"* and to present afresh, through the atoning Lamb, her body, soul, and spirit, with all her redeemed powers, to God; in order that her whole existence, by being thus renewedly laid upon the altar, might be ready for the Master's use in any department of labor to which he might appoint her, whether in her family or in the world.

And here it might be well to state in reference to the members of her household, she proved that it was not an unmeaning service to follow in the footsteps of God's ancient servant Job, who arose early and bore the individual members of his family before the mercy-seat, by presenting the offerings, ordained by God, in their behalf, in order, through this medium, to crave the acceptance of their persons. Even thus she found it to be a very satisfactory exercise, to present, through the merits of the sin-atoning Sacrifice, not only her own soul, but also the case of each individual member, imploring for them individually that they might be permitted, through the merits of Christ, to abide as in the presence of God, under the direct rays of the Sun of righteousness, during the day.

And often had she reason to observe throughout the day, that not only the members of her household, but also her house, which had also been specially consecrated to God, were held under a divine influence, and the Spirit,

"Which, as a peaceful dove,
Flies the abode of noise and strife,"

was felt to be brooding over that household, in answer to the supplications of the early hour. Thus prepared to spend the day in the peaceful presence of God, they loved, when assembled around the family altar, to sing, —

"How happy, gracious Lord, are we,
Divinely drawn to follow thee
    Whose hours divided are
Between the mount and multitude,
Our days are spent in doing good,
    Our nights in praise and prayer.

"With us no melancholy void,
No moments linger unemploy'd,
    Or unimproved below;
Our weariness of life is gone,
Who live to serve our God alone,
    And only thee to know.

The winter's night and summer's day
Glide imperceptibly away,
    Too short to sing thy praise;
Too few we find the happy hours,
And haste to join the heavenly powers
    In everlasting lays.

"With all who chant thy name on high,
And holy, holy, holy, cry,
    A bright harmonious throng,
We long thy praises to repeat,
And ceaseless sing around thy seat
    The new eternal song."

It was a prayer frequently presented, that the Spirit might so urge her onward, that she might not be permitted to rest short of any state of grace made possible by the death, and the present intercession of the Savior.

She believed it to be a duty imposed by the highest obligation of love, on all professed followers of the Lord Jesus, to endeavor, by all possible means, to give faithful representation in their *individual experience* of the power of grace to transform to the uttermost.

The weight of responsibility resting upon those who lower the standard, by an unfaithful representation, either by the living epistle of an unholy life, verbally, or in written communications, she saw to be so tremendous, that she was assured eternity alone could determine, its fearful magnitude.

She believed, in accordance with Scripture testimony, the sentiment comprehensively expressed by a recent writer, "Christ has taken glorified humanity to heaven, in order to represent us before the throne of mercy, and hath left his followers to be his representatives on earth;" and she verily believed that much of the infidelity, depopulating God's fair dominions, and so rapidly peopling the regions of despair, is owing to the untrue representation in life and sentiments given by a vast majority of unholy professors. That infidelity is the consequence resulting from these failures, and the correctness of the allusion just given, she saw to be directly inferred from the words of the Savior, John xvii, 21-23.

It was in view of these tremendous responsibilities that she so greatly desired to be urged onward by the persuasions of the Spirit, in order that she might apprehend that for which she had been apprehended by Christ, "and be able to give before the world a fair exhibition, in every department of life, of whatsoever things are honest, lovely, pure, and of good report. And in her domestic relations, as well as in those termed more spiritual duties, she often prayerfully presented the inquiry,

"But where can I resemble thee,
    And in thy God-like nature share?
Thy humble follower let me be,
    Thy blessed likeness let me bear.

"Pure may I be, averse to sin,
    Just, holy, merciful, and true,
And let *thine image form'd within,*
    Shine out in all I say or do."

When she first made up her mind that every earthly consideration should be in the highest degree subservient to the prominent object of attaining the witness of *entire consecration,* she had no other expectation than that of entering heart and soul into her earthly cares again, for the Lord had written this lesson upon her heart, "He that careth not for his own household is worse than an infidel;" and she did not, at this interesting point of her experience, intend to neglect them, but only resolved that they should cease to be *absorbing* until this assurance was gained; and it was at this precise point in her pilgrimage that Almighty grace gained a signal victory over a naturally over-anxious spirit.

She never afterward saw it necessary to enter heart and soul into the otherwise vexatious cares with which the mother of every family is surrounded, but found, after having chosen with her whole soul "the better part," that she could ever sing, —

"Lo, I come with joy to do
   My blessed Master's will:
Him in outward works pursue,
   And serve his pleasure still.
Faithful to my Lord's commands,
   I still would choose" the better part,
Serve with careful Martha's hands
   And loving Mary's heart.

"Careful without care I am,
   Nor feel the happy toil;
Kept in peace by Jesus' name,
   Supported by his smile;
Joyful thus my faith to show,
   I find his service my reward,
Every work I do below,
   I do it to the Lord."

And yet she never regarded a minute observance of the admonition, "Whatsoever things are true, honest, just, *pure, lovely, and of good report,*" as more sacredly and scrupulously binding than from the period when the resolution was made that they should *cease to be absorbing*.

From that time she felt that the honor of God was as much concerned in judicious, external and internal household arrangements, as in closet duties. By the effective, pure, and lovely order and symmetry pervading all the works of God, she felt that man was being taught an ever-speaking and ever-enduring lesson.

But by a careful attention to the instructions of the blessed word, she found that much which had formerly augmented her cares was easily to be dispensed with, without any infringement either on the happiness of others or her own; and in many respects these omissions increased the happiness of all. Take, for instance, the admonition contained in the prophetic sentiment, "In that day shall there be upon the bells of the horses, HOLINESS UNTO THE LORD, and the pots in the Lord's house shall be like the bowls before the altar: yea, every pot in Jerusalem and in Judea shall be HOLINESS TO THE LORD OF HOSTS."

By this she observed that there was nothing with which she had a right to do that was either *too high* or *too low* to be inscribed with "HOLINESS UNTO THE LORD;" and she resolved not to give her approval to, or to permit her time to be absorbed with, any pursuit that would not unequivocally bear this inscription. And she gained, beyond all calculation, by resolving not to venture on questionable ground in reference to these things.

"O! I wish I could always be as happy as you are," said an aged professor to her one day. She felt deeply humbled by the observation, and hardly knew what to say in reply, thinking that to disclose the secret of her happiness would be to reprove the aged sister. But on looking to God, she felt it was required that she should say, to the glory of grace, "that she did not dare to be otherwise than happy," because she believed one command to be equally as binding as another. God had said, "Be careful for nothing, but in *everything* by prayer and supplication, with *thanksgiving,* let your requests be made known to God, and the peace of God, which passeth all understanding, shall keep your hearts and minds through Christ Jesus." "The Lord knew," she continued to say, "that we should have cares, otherwise he would not have made provision for the disposal of them as he has done, by inviting us to cast all our care upon him, with the assurance that he careth for us, thereby empowering us to comply with the requirement, rejoice evermore, pray without ceasing, and in everything give thanks." And she felt that these divine requisitions could not be complied with, without taking the most minute things, as well as those regarded as of the greatest magnitude, to God. It was her habit to decide the matter thus: "Is this of as much consequence to me as a hair of my head? If so, I will make my request known unto Him who hath said, 'The very hairs of your head are numbered.'"

Chapter Five

"That the trial of your faith being much more precious than that of gold that perisheth, though it be tried with fire, might be found to be unto praise, and glory, and honor, at the appearing of Jesus Christ." — *Peter.*

One day, after having given to a friend a narration of the way by which the Lord had brought her, and stated a variety of experience, trials by the way, and the manner in which she had been enabled to overcome them, the friend remarked something expressive of surprise and gratitude in reference to the Lord's instructive dealings. "O," said she, in return, "this is the way the Lord takes to instruct and discipline his children. That which is learned by experience is much more deeply written upon the heart than what is learned by mere precept. By this painful process, the lessons of grace remain written in living characters upon the mind, and we are better able to tell to travelers coming after us, just how and where we met with this and the other difficulty, how we overcame, and the peculiar lessons learned by passing through *this* and *that* trial, and thus be not only advantaged in our own experience, but helpful to our fellow-pilgrims."

Scarcely had she finished speaking, when the prayer that she might be made a monument of the extent of saving grace to transform the heart and life was brought by the Spirit to her remembrance, and the inquiry was presented whether she would be willing that the petition should be granted, if in order for its accomplishment, it were needful that she should be called to pass through trials unheard of in magnitude and duration?

An unutterable weight of responsibility rested upon her mind, and she hastened to prostrate herself in solitude before God. She felt that it was an inquiry proposed by the Spirit that searcheth all things, and was assured that the decision of that hour would tell momentously on her eternal destiny.

She thought of the various, complicated, and lengthened trials, transmitted by the inspired page, also those that had met her eye and ear, most formidable in magnitude and duration, and after having weighed the matter, that she might not ask to be baptized with a baptism that she was not able to bear, prostrate on her face before the Sovereign of heaven and earth she said, "O Lord, I now renewedly give myself into thy hands, as clay in the hands of the potter, in order that thy whole will and pleasure may be accomplished in me. Let the petition be answered. Let thy power be manifested to transform and save to the uttermost, though trials of inconceivable magnitude may await me. I rely upon thy faithfulness. Thou hast promised that I shall not be tempted above that which I am able to bear. But if thou seest, at any time, my faith about to fail, remove the trial, or cut short the work in righteousness, and take me home to thyself: suffer me not to live to dishonor thee."

The seal, proclaiming her wholly the Lord's, was now more deeply enstamped, and she realized from that hour that she was taken more closely to the embrace of Infinite Love, and had cast anchor deeper within the veil. Ever afterward, in passing through the most painful, complex trials, she found a blessed satisfaction in referring to this period when she had so fully counted the cost.

In reference to religious associations, and early culture, being taught from a child to know the Scriptures, and made familiar with the writings and experience of those who had, in generations passed away, been lights in the religious firmament, and in more mature life favored with the pious example and precept of a true yoke-fellow in the gospel, with the numerous advantages resulting from being thus favorably circumstanced, it might indeed be said that the lines had fallen to her in pleasant places, yet she proved,' notwithstanding all these gracious considerations, that the "servant is not above his Master."

Yes, she was called to endure trials. To the observation of those unacquainted with the Christian warfare such a statement could hardly be understood or accredited. Consequently, the number of those who knew *just how* to sympathize was not great. Probably for this reason, in part, she seemed seldom called to dwell upon the particulars of those deep mental conflicts which she was permitted to endure, when she was called to wrestle, not against flesh and blood, but against principalities and powers, &c.

These mighty conflicts were repeated yet again and again, and through each succeeding year of her pilgrimage: with each conflict it seemed, while engaged in the contest, as though it had reached the summit of human endurance, yet the succeeding one was found to be proportionate in magnitude to the increase of strength that had been gained by the former trial, and the intermediate interval for growth, and knowledge, and spiritual stature.

These trials, though they sometimes arose from outward causes, were generally inward, and the struggle they caused is indescribable; in the midst of which she was often called to lean so entirely, "with *naked* faith, upon a *naked* promise," that nature was sometimes tempted in its shrinkings to say, "My God, why hast thou forsaken me?" but still holding with an unyielding grasp upon the promise, "I will never leave nor forsake thee." And believing that the Savior was treading "the wine-press alone, and of the people there was none with him," when he gave utterance to this expression, she was checked ere she had given words to the thought, and instead of indulging in those words, which none but He who

"Wept that man might smile,"

need use, she said in the language of faith, "My God, thou hast not forsaken me."

Chapter Six

"That ye may know the way by which ye must go: for ye have not passed this way heretofore." — *Joshua*.

"Patient the appointed race to run,
    This weary world we cast aside
From strength to strength we travel on,
    The New Jerusalem to find.
Our labor this, our only aim,
To find the New Jerusalem."

She verily believed that the entire course of the traveler journeying to the heavenly city may be onward and upward.

"Ye have to pass a way that ye have not passed heretofore," said the courageous Joshua to the unbelieving Jews, who had been forty years accomplishing in zig-zag, and almost aimless wanderings, a journey that might have been performed in fewer days than they had taken years. It was thus, she conceived, that many professed followers of Jesus, in consequence of unbelief, necessarily ending in disobedience, are years in accomplishing that which might have been performed in fewer days.

She could find no Scriptural reason, why each successive day might not witness the heavenly traveler at a higher point of elevation in his homeward course than the day previous, and she felt confident that there should not be a perfect rest of spirit, without this assurance. In the early part of her career in the way of holiness, she resolved not to be satisfied without knowing that she was thus making daily advances in the knowledge and love of God — "the way of holiness."

She was much encouraged when about to start in the way by an observation from one who had made considerable progress. "More," said he, "is to be gained by *one act of faith,* than could be accomplished by years of painful toiling *without* it." The justness of this statement she had cause to observe, not only from a review of her own experience, but also strikingly exhibited in a variety of instances which came under her observation.

"O!" said one of Christ's little ones to her one day, who had but three days before received the Spirit of adoption, "I feel as if I could not rest short of anything which it is my privilege to enjoy." This was at the close of a social meeting, where the witnesses had just been testifying of the efficacy of the blood of Jesus to cleanse from all unrighteousness. "I feel," she continued to say, "that I want to be holy — I *must be holy!*"

The sister assured her in reply that the very desire for this blessing was a sure intimation, of not only the willingness, but the intention of God to give it, and that it was only for her to persevere in looking for it, in order speedily to obtain it.

She returned home — wrestled with God Jacob-like during the night, and about nine o'clock the next morning came off a prevailing Israel. Having found the pearl, she ran with intense eagerness to tell of the power of saving grace to "sanctify throughout body, soul, and spirit," and the fruits, that were at once and continuously apparent, gave abundant testimony to the genuineness of the work.

At another time, on meeting with a youthful disciple, the friend who introduced him to the notice of this child of Jesus, said by way of introduction, "This is one of the lambs of the flock." On addressing herself to him she said, "Brother, I am told that you are one of the lambs of the flock, and as such, did you ever think what a sweet resting place you have! You know, Jesus carries the lambs in his bosom, and now what may you not ask with the expectation of receiving? Surely he now says to you, 'Ask what ye will, and it shall be done unto you.'"

He expressed a longing desire for holiness, and felt that he could not be fully prepared for every good word and work without it. She told him the Almighty Savior loved him so well, that when on earth it was not too much for him to spend the whole night in prayer on a special occasion, and asked whether he felt the need of the blessing enough to be willing to do likewise. She then related, for his admonition and encouragement, the case of the Canaanitish woman — the seeming inattention of the blessed Savior — the discouraging observation of the disciples — the apparent repulsiveness of the allusion, "It is not meet to take the children's bread, and to cast it to dogs."

She assured him that this was permitted for the trial of the faith of this woman, and that the blessed Savior's heart was doubtless all the time melting with love and desire to impart to her the desire of her heart, but was only waiting to make her an honorable example to all succeeding generations of victorious faith, perseverance, and humility.

He concluded to wrestle with God until the blessing was given, notwithstanding he might at first seem to be repulsed; and about two or three hours afterward, while crying, Lord, *sanctify me now!* the blessing was given in such power, that body and soul were overwhelmed with the divine presence and glory. Another brother, who had, during a meeting for social worship, expressed a strong desire to be fully conformed to the will of God in all things, was asked by this sister, on returning from the meeting, whether he was really so much in earnest on the subject of holiness, that he would be willing to make a present effort for the attainment of it, by spending a little time in conversing, and in making an effort to obtain it *by faith*. He replied that he would be willing to try all night if he thought it would do any good.

She referred to the sacrifice that God required of Abraham, Gen. xv, 7-19; and the assurance that Abraham must have had in his own mind of the *intention* of God to accept an offering that he had himself demanded. The brother acknowledged the reasonableness of Abraham's faith, and also the manner in which God would have been dishonored had he dared to doubt the ultimate acceptance of his sacrifice, notwithstanding the heavenly fire was so long delayed.

She then assured him that God, just at that moment, was demanding a sacrifice at his hand. He had, also, most explicitly pointed out the nature of that sacrifice, and was now beseeching, by the voice of his word, that he should present it. See Rom. xii, 1.

She asked whether he was willing to sacrifice body, soul, and spirit upon the Lord's altar, a *living* sacrifice, never to be resumed. He replied, "Yes." "But when will you do it?" said the sister. "By the help of the Lord, I will do it now," he replied. A pause of intense interest ensued, when the sister, perceiving that another step must be taken ere he had entered, said, "But, brother, do you *do it* now?" A moment of hesitation, and he exclaimed, "Yes, glory be to God, I do! I DO!" and with most joyful lips he began to rejoice in Christ as his full Savior; and continues, to the present day, a joyful traveler in the King's highway.

On one occasion, a brother, who had been, for some time, endeavoring to have his goings established in the "way of holiness," expressed himself as quite confident of having laid all upon the altar. "And will not God receive the offering!" asked the sister. "I have no other evidence than his word," he replied. "And is not *that sufficient?*" said the sister, surprised at his incredulity. "What! believe with no *other* evidence?" he exclaimed. Wounded at the evident, though unintentional, lightness with which the authority of the blessed word was regarded, she gave her views, in answer to the last inquiry, thus: "Suppose, brother, you should call in with a much-loved friend, in whom you had the most unbounded confidence; you begin to make a statement of some circumstances in which I am greatly interested; when through with the narration, I say, 'And how do you *know* this to be so? What *evidence* have you of its truth!' With an air of satisfaction and confidence, you turn to your friend and say, 'My friend saw the whole transaction, and informed me of it.' With disappointment I exclaim, 'Why, brother, is that the only way you know of it? Have you no other *evidence?*' Would you not feel grieved, and think I had *greatly dishonored your friend?*" The brother burst into tears, and replied, "O! I never thought of unbelief in that way before. My sin has found me out!"

Chapter Seven

"He that rejecteth me and receiveth not my words, hath ONE that judgeth him: the word that I have spoken the same shall judge him in the last day." — *The Savior.*

"The Lord seems to have one peculiar way of leading me onward, in all my experience," said this traveler, while conversing, on one occasion, with one who desired instruction in reference to getting into the "way of holiness."

"I have been called, in the first place," she continued to say, "to take the WORD OF THE LORD, to examine myself by its tests, and just so far as I have found its promises suited to my condition, just so far I have rested, most confidently, upon its truths. And having previously made the resolution that, if possessed of these tests, I would venture, whether my *feelings* warranted the conclusion or not, assured that heaven and earth shall pass away before one jot or tittle of all that he hath said shall fail; I have invariably found that, just so soon as I have made the venture, the foundation upon which I rested was as *firm as the pillars of eternity!*"

While repeating the words last mentioned, relative to the firmness of her foundation, stronger conviction of the Scriptural propriety of the course she had been divinely impelled to pursue, than she ever before felt, was imparted, and with this, a sudden and vivid recollection of a dream, which she had several years previously, which, during the intervening years, seemed to have been entirely forgotten, but which now, with the freshness of yesterday, passed before her. "O!" she exclaimed, "I had such a singular dream, four or five years since, which was *precisely prophetical* of what has since been my experience.

"It was this: I thought my spirit had left the body, and entered the spiritual world; I found everything there very unlike what I had before conjectured. 'What state is this?' I inquired. 'This is the middle state,' was the reply. 'The middle state!' said I, 'why, they say, on earth, there is no middle state." [1]

'They have a great many strange conjectures.' on earth, such as they have *no foundation for from the word of God,*' was the answer. 'And what is to be my state here?' I eagerly inquired. 'Your state!' said the spirit, chidingly, 'why, you have had the BIBLE — the WORD OF THE LORD — and by this you should have tried yourself, and have known what your state was before you came here; but since you have it no more with you, if you can think of but *one passage* by which to test yourself, you may just as well know what your state will be *now,* as by leaving it till you are called before your Judge, *for it is by this you are to be judged.*'

"Never before did I have such a view of the infinite importance and eternal bearing of the WORD of GOD; I saw that it was in verity as truly the word of the Lord, as though audibly uttered from the heavens, and thus arresting continuously the outward ear, as well as the inward perceptions of mortals.

"I thought of the various denominations in the world that I had left, who, in expressing their doctrinal peculiarities, would say, 'I believe so,' and another, 'I believe so,' and thought, 'O! why did not every one run, with Bible in hand, raised aloft, crying, "The BIBLE says so! The BIBLE says so?"'

"But the all-absorbing, unutterable desire of my heart now was, to bring to remembrance some passage by which to try myself. Yet the overwhelming consideration, that all was now past change, and that my eternal destiny was pending on the decision to be thus made, seemed so momentous, that the uncertainty of one minute was unendurable. The intense anxiety and hurry of my spirit to bring to remembrance some passage by which the point might be decided were too much for the fluttering spirit while still incased in the body, and in its strugglings, it awoke to the consciousness that it was still with the body, on the shores of time."

At the time when this dream occurred, her mind had been under an unusual influence for several days. She had withdrawn her attention, as far as possible, from everything that might divide its purposes, and centered it in the aim to get an assurance that she was a child of God, in some such *luminous* or *extraordinary* manner that there never might be a shade of plausibility in the temptation to doubt.

But, notwithstanding the many toilsome hours thus spent, she seemed to come no nearer the mark than when she began. And it was while engaged in these apparently fruitless endeavors that she had the dream alluded to. It has since been cause of astonishment that the lesson, so evidently intended to be communicated, was not apprehended. It seemed to be regarded at the time as merely admonitory, that she was about to exchange worlds.

From views of the unseen world, other than those mentioned, assurance took possession of her mind, that she had been permitted to take a glance into the spiritual world. Views of its realities, both Scriptural and rational, were brought abidingly within the range of her perceptions, unlike anything of which she had ever before had any conception. Within a few weeks after its occurrence, she often resolved on noting it down, but was driven back from the pursuit by a shrinking persuasiveness that she was dealing with spiritual things.

After a few months the recollection of it seemed to have passed away, so that it did not return to memory for years, until it was so vividly presented on the occasion stated.

The intervening experience, to which special allusion was made when spoken of as "prophetical," was this: The "prize of holiness" had been presented to her mind by the dictations of the blessed word, as an attainment, toward which every redeemed one should not only *aspire,* but which he should also possess — the rightful heritage of the believer.

Yet, whenever her aspirations were the most ardent, the suggestion was the most powerful, that it were better to be *thorough* in "the principles of the doctrine of Christ" *first,* before going on unto perfection.

This was so repeatedly, or continuously, the case that she began to see the suggestion calculated to keep her ever toiling at first principles, forbidding, most effectively, an onward progress in the school of Christ.

About this time "Philips' Guides" came under her observation, and she was greatly encouraged by some Scriptural advice given to those similarly exercised with herself, and pursuant to counsel there given, resolved, and most solemnly covenanted with God, that if there were *but one* passage in his WORD by which she might test herself, and know that she was a new creature, she would *never doubt again;* but would resolutely believe irrespective of frames and feelings.

She then took, this passage, "As many as are led by the Spirit of God, they are the sons of God." Previous to this, she had taken as the motto of life, "*Entire devotion of heart and life to God.*" She now asked, What has induced this resolution and led to corresponding action? "The Spirit of God," was the reply. And this was the most conclusive answer to each inquiry, after having made a minute examination, of the motives impelling her to action. Knowledge sufficiently convincing for the full establishment of her faith, assuring her that she was a child of God, from this time beamed upon her mind. Most truly might it now be said, -

"Meridian evidence puts doubt to flight."

Not one temptation, bearing a shade of plausibility, was ever, from that hour, presented to her mind, to doubt her adoption into the family of Christ. And now she greatly rejoiced, that. God had so long borne with her, in bringing her to this point. On retracing all the way that the Lord had brought her from infancy, she observed that the urgings of his Spirit had been persuasively directing her mind away from the uncertain traditions and example of the fallible creature, to the only INFALLIBLE STANDARD — the ONE STANDARD of the only wise God — ever appealing as a voice from the throne of the ETERNAL, saying, "THERE IN ONE THAT JUDGETH YOU THE WORD THAT I HAVE SPOKEN, THE SAME SHALL JUDGE YOU AT THE LAST DAY."

The wisdom of this MIGHTY COUNSELOR, which she from this period took yet more closely to the companionship of her heart, in no part of her heavenward course seemed more apparent than in the manner in which she became confirmed in this assurance of divine relationship. Had she depended on merely joyous emotions for this witness, when those emotions had subsided, and she was required to walk by faith, the witness would have fled with the emotion. But here the blessed WORD ever stood the same.

It was but to know that those tests of divine relationship were still maintained in her own heart, in order to be assured that it was still her privilege, though in heaviness, through manifold temptations, to rejoice in the confidence that there was the same sure word of prophecy, even the WORD of Him "with whom there is no variableness, neither shadow of turning," upon which to repose; resting here, well might she, with an unutterable degree of confidence, proclaim the foundation *firm as the pillars of eternity.*

[1] The allusion was to the well-known words,......

"A heaven and hell, and that alone
  Beyond the present time is known;
There is no middle state."

The sentiment contained in which is not at all at variance with the views at this time received.

Chapter Eight

"Therefore, leaving the principles of the doctrine of Christ, let us go on unto perfection; not laying again the foundation of repentance from dead works, and of faith toward God."

"Soul! now know thy full salvation;
  Rise o'er sin, and fear, and, care;
Joy to know in every station
  Something still to do or bear.
Think what Spirit dwells within thee,
  Think what Father's smiles are thine;
Think that Jesus died to win thee;
  Child of heaven! caust thou repine?

"Haste thee on from grace to glory,
  Arm'd by faith, and wing'd by prayer;
Heaven's eternal day's before thee,
  God's own hand shall lead thee there.
Soon shall close thy earthly mission,
  Soon shall end thy pilgrim days;

Hope shall end in full fruition,
   Faith in sight, and prayer in praise."

But little progress, comparatively, was gained by her almost unceasing efforts to advance in the heavenly way, until the successful endeavor, just glanced at, was made; from that period, through the omnipotence of faith, she gained daily victories over the world, the flesh, and Satan.

One of the most signal victories obtained immediately subsequent to the experience just stated was at a meeting for social worship. A few disciples, whom grace had empowered to testify in experimental verity of Christ as a full Savior, had given testimony to that effect. A view of the impartiality of God in dispensing his favors flashed across her mind with such power, that her heart exclaimed with Peter, "Of a truth, I perceive that God is no respecter of persons."

At once she began to reflect thus: If I am but willing to make use of the same means, for the attainment of the same state of grace which these friends profess, God will surely give it to me.

She then formed the resolve that she would make use of *every possible* means for the attainment of the blessing. In doing this she felt the sacred responsibility of having lifted her hand to God, and immediately, on an opportunity offering, she proved the sincerity of her heart by acting correspondingly.

In making a frank statement of the views and intention that had just been influencing her mind, she felt that a snare was at once broken which had bound her for years. The duty of making confession with the mouth had stood before her of all duties the most formidable; but she now formed the resolution, that if she should literally die in the struggle to overcome nature, she would be a martyr in the effort, rather than that Satan should triumph.

A victory that told advantageously on all the subsequent pilgrimage of life was here gained, and the progressive steps were now rapidly taken by which she was led into the King's highway.

Aware of the proneness of the heart to forget the admonition divinely enjoined, "Thou shalt remember all the way which the Lord thy God hath led thee...in the wilderness, to humble thee and prove thee," she resolved from that time to be more diligent in noting down, for future remembrance, the Spirit's gracious leadings, some of which stand briefly recorded as follows:

Feb. 23, 18 —. For some days past my soul has been longing after God; I have been waiting at Jerusalem for the promise of the Father; blessed be God the Father, the Son, and the Holy Ghost, that my waiting has not been in vain; my faith has been as the dawning of the morning, clearer and yet clearer; and now the calm sunshine of God's presence illuminates my soul.

The precious words, "whereby are given unto us exceeding great and precious promises, that by these ye might be partakers of the divine nature," were applied to my soul with much power this evening. Yes, I saw such comprehensiveness and depth of meaning in them, as I had never before apprehended. What! am I to be made a partaker of the divine nature! Shout, O heavens! be glad, O earth!

And shall I indeed, even I, who have been so fearful and unbelieving, be yet able to comprehend, with all saints, what is the length, breadth, depth, and height of the love of Christ? Shall I know the perfect love of God which passeth knowledge, and be filled with the fullness of God?

Yes! I shall be changed from glory to glory, until I shall be made like unto his own glorious image. Glorious hope! The faith of assurance tells me it shall be so.

I never before felt so truly as though all in Christ were mine. He who withheld not his own Son, will not withhold any good thing from me. Henceforth, O Lord, I covenant afresh, to devote all my powers more decidedly than ever to thy reasonable service. Wilt thou accept the offering, O my Savior and my Redeemer? If so, O let me feel from this moment that the sacrifice is received. O that to me the power were given, not to live one moment longer to myself! May my all, consecrated to thee from this hour, in the strictest sense, glorify thee!

I would that the time past should suffice, in which I have been so ungrateful as not to render thee a whole-hearted service. Praised be the Lord, my strength and righteousness, that he has honored me of late, by permitting me to bear his hallowed cross. I will now, through grace, choose it as cause of my greatest glorying. Lord, strengthen me: I am weak, but thou art everlasting strength, and thou art my portion.

Feb. 24. I have often felt as though God had called me peculiarly to a life of holiness. I have also felt that in order to be led in this way, the path of self-denial must be mine. Well, thanks be to God that he has given me, in a gracious degree, a disposition to walk in the way of his appointment. From the depth of my heart I can say, through grace, that I have deliberately chosen to walk in the more excellent way, even though the highway to it may be by passing through trials most contrary to nature. I know that my heavenly Father loves me. He will not require me to do anything but what will be eventually for my good and the glory of his great name. And is it not my greatest desire that his name should be glorified? Then let me not shun the cross. If, by following the motions of his Spirit, I can win souls to Christ, and thus lay up treasure in heaven, shall motives of mere worldly prudence, unsanctioned by grace, deter me? Shall I lean to my own understanding, when he has declared that the wisdom of this world is foolishness with him? Rather let me tread onward in the footsteps of Him who was a "man of sorrows, and acquainted with grief."

Feb. 27. Glory be to God that I have this day been enabled to resolve to follow the faith of Abraham, who, against hope, believed in hope. I now repose in the promises of the unchangeable Jehovah, believing that what he has promised he is fully able to perform. His promises are all yea and amen in Christ Jesus. O may I never rest till I have the witness of the Spirit, that my heart is the temple of an indwelling God, and have the full confidence that Christ reigns supreme on the throne of my affections, bringing every thought into obedience to himself.

This is the blessing which I fully believe God has in reserve for me; "for this my cry shall never cease." For several days past the eye of my faith has been so intensely fixed on this point, that almost every breath has been a breathing after it. O Lord, make me holy! establish fully with me the new covenant. Thou hast said, "I will sprinkle you with clean water, and ye shall be clean: from all your filthiness and from all your idols will I cleanse you."

I feel that I have been greatly deficient, and have lost inconceivably, by not exercising that faith which takes God at his word; that faith which is apprehended in the simple illustration, "God hath said it, and I believe it." When looked at in this light, O, how exceedingly sinful does unbelief appear! Doubt the veracity of the immutable Jehovah! Shall I, a worm of earth, dare doubt the word of the omnipotent God? Shall I look upward and ask the fulfillment of a promise, with a feeling of hesitation whether God will fulfill his word? Spirit of eternal truth, forbid it. Lord Jesus, make me strong in faith.

June 17. I have of late been enabled, by the help of the Spirit, to improve in experience, and I have found it good to appeal to Him who can be touched with the feelings of my infirmities. He knows the strength and sincerity of my desires to serve him fully. I have been pleading the promise, "They shall all be taught of God." I triumph in the expectation that I shall be enabled, through the Spirit's influence, to perfect holiness in the fear of God.

I have placed the standard of Christian excellence high, and have asked strength of Omnipotence to be enabled to reach the summit of my desires. "My heart is fixed! O, God, my heart is fixed!" and, though the opposition of a perverse will, the infirmities of nature, or crosses indescribably varied, may oppose, my progress, I trust, will yet, through grace, be onward and upward. I long to be made a monument of what the grace of God can effect on a once rebellious child of Adam. O! this, I am sure, is a holy ambition, and authorized by Scripture. I have been enabled to spend much time in secret prayer this week, and I feel that I have received a new degree of strength for the holy effort; but O, how little to what I might have received, had my faith been more active and persevering! Lord, increase my faith, and enable me ever to go on from strength to strength.

June 18. Of late I have increasingly felt the importance of time. In view of an eternal state of existence, and the short space allotted for its vast concernments, I do indeed feel the force of the admonition, "What thy hand findeth to do, do it with thy might."

"Short is our longest day of life,
   And soon its prospect ends;
Yet on this day's uncertain date
   Eternity depends.

> "Yet equal to our being's aim,
>   The space to mortals given;
> *And every moment, well improved,*
>   *Secures an age in heaven!"*

How important, then, that every eternity-winged moment should bear to the abodes of immortality just such a report as may best bear a reviewal in the clear light of eternity.

I have thought that some rules for the regulation of my time, and the distribution of my duties, might be helpful. I will endeavor to rise at four: spend from four to six in reading the Scriptures, and other devotional exercise: half an hour for closet duties at midday. I will resolve, at this season, to bear in special remembrance those who have said, "Pray for me," not forgetting the exhortation, I Tim. ii, 1. If practicable I will get an hour to spend with God at the close of the day.

In order to keep a continuous and comprehensive arrangement of Bible truth before my mind, I will resolve to pursue a systematic course of reading. I purpose to read, in proper connection, in the Old Testament in the morning; in the Gospels at noon, and in the Epistles in the evening. This I will endeavor to do, with the most careful circumspection, inasmuch as God hath said, "*Search* the Scriptures;" "*Study* to show thyself approved."

If I meet with portions which I cannot readily comprehend, I will, through grace, seek diligently and go *confidently* unto Him who hath said, "I will instruct thee," believing it is his *will* that I should learn some special lesson of grace from every portion of his word, whether historical or from those parts deemed more practical.

Resolved that the young persons in my Bible class shall be daily remembered in my stated approaches unto God. I would also here most solemnly register my purpose that I will, in the strength of the Lord, endeavor to take up every cross, and, through grace, *never* shun it, when convinced of duty, but take it up in the name of the Lord, and trust him for the consequences; also that the attainment of a clear *Scriptural faith* shall be most prominent in my petitions before the Lord. This I regard as a fundamental principle in a life of devotion. Each morning shall also witness a renewed dedication of *all* my redeemed powers to the Father, Son, and Holy Spirit; still further resolved, I will unceasingly aim at *entire* devotion of heart and life to God. The Lord help me in the performance of these resolutions.

June 24. In consequence of ill health I have not been able to observe all the resolutions in my last; an alteration in domestic arrangements has also, in a measure, frustrated my purposes; I regret that I do not, with greater equanimity of feeling, bear the thwarting of my purposes. O, how much I need establishing grace! I know — O! yes, I *feel* that it is, in all its richest plenitude, for me; and yet I live without it. O! when shall my heart be circumcised to love the Lord my God with all my heart?

July 27. The Lord reigns unrivaled in my heart; he has my supreme affections: for some days past I have experienced such a heartfelt want of the assurance of being cleansed from all unrighteousness, to know that the motives influencing every thought, word, and action, originate from a pure fountain, that I last evening resolved I could no longer do without it. Between the hours of eight and nine — while pleading at the throne of grace for a present fulfillment of the exceeding great and precious promises; pleading also the fullness and freeness of the atonement, its unbounded efficacy, and making an entire surrender of body, soul, and spirit; time, talents, and influence; and also of the dearest ties of nature, my beloved husband and child; in a word, my earthly *all — I received the assurance that God the Father, through the atoning Lamb, accepted the sacrifice;* my heart was emptied of self, and cleansed of all idols, from all filthiness of the flesh and spirit, and I realized that I dwelt in God, and felt that he had become the portion of my soul, my ALL in ALL.

Since which, though I have been exercised by many temptations to question the extent of the work, yet, blessed be God, they have been but temptations. The Spirit of the Lord hath raised up a standard against Satan, and I rejoice in the assurance that more are they that are for me than all that be against me.

My faith in the reality of the work grows stronger; I feel that, instead of its being presumptuous to believe, it would greatly grieve the Spirit of my condescending Savior were I to doubt the all-sufficiency of his grace to sustain me in the full enjoyment of this blessing. Glory be to the Father! glory be to the Son! glory be to the Holy Spirit! my Triune God! my all in all.

As my heart has been of late much drawn out after God in the night season, for this inestimable blessing, even when my bodily powers have been under the influence of sleep, my expectations were much raised last night, and almost my last thoughts, ere I gave myself to sleep, were, that the Lord would manifest himself much more gloriously. What was my surprise, on awaking, in a most frightful dream! I thought I was standing in the back room, when a loud knock was given at the door: from the unseasonableness of the hour, (being about eleven,) and the knowledge that all the inlets of the house had been some time previously secured, I knew that something must be wrong; but aware that I was equally in the power of the intruder whether I said, "Come in," or otherwise; I firmly said, "Come in;" when a personage, of more ferocious countenance and more fiend-like in every particular than anything I had ever witnessed, came in. "Is the — in?" he demanded, in a very authoritative tone. "He is in the front room, on the sofa," I replied, thinking that, as he passed through the folding doors, I could run behind him and give the alarm to the house, ere any injury had happened my dear husband. In the effort to scream for assistance, I awoke.

It was suggested, "You were expecting some unusual manifestation for the further establishment of your faith, and yet where is even your usual tranquility and breathing after God? Is this not enough to convince you that you were mistaken in the exercises of last evening?" There was something so taunting and fiendish in the whole matter, that I was sure it must be Satan, and as I had resolved that I would not parley with him one moment, aware that I had no power nor wisdom to contend with an enemy so exceedingly subtle, I gave the whole matter over into the care of my covenant-keeping God, and again sunk sweetly to repose in the arms of Almighty Love.

About an hour or two afterward, I again awoke: but, O! the change — I was aroused by an inward voice, saying, "Behold! I, an angel, beseech you that ye walk worthy of the vocation whereunto ye are called." "An angel! an angel!" said I, aware that it was not the exact phraseology of Scripture. With these words I awoke, and, O, how my soul did exult in Christ as my *full,* my complete Savior! I was reminded of the blessed Savior's temptation in the wilderness; also of the angels that afterward came and ministered unto him. The witness was now given, with indisputable clearness, that I had not believed in vain; the full tide of joy flowed into my soul.

My beloved husband, who had been some months past in the enjoyment of this blessing, came in just after I had risen from my knees, returning thanks for the manifestation just received. He had been from home on professional business, since the evening previous, and had not heard of the manner in which God had blessed me; and when I related to him the exercises of the preceding evening, the way in which Satan had tried to disturb my peace, and the manifestation just received, he rejoiced with a joy unspeakable and full of glory. Amazing condescension! I cannot find words to express my views of the blessedness of this great salvation.

July 31. Still the Lord is with me: my contests have been severe with the powers of darkness; but the Lord my Redeemer hath strengthened me, and I have more than conquered; I have obtained a much greater increase of faith, and the Lord has, in much mercy, established my goings beyond my expectations; I feel that he is hourly establishing his kingdom of righteousness, peace, and joy in the Holy Ghost, more firmly in my heart.

Yesterday and today the hand of the enemy has been, in a great measure, stayed, and the Comforter has said to my soul, -

"Israel now shall dwell alone,
  With Jesus in his heart."

Glorious hope! O how my soul exults in it!

As the duties of the Sabbath have of late been rather arduous, I had been led, from this and other considerations, to think that temptations would abound, and I earnestly entreated God for strength to resist; but, O, how delightfully did I realize that my enemies were all gone! Never before did I so fully enjoy the presence of an indwelling God: since which my heritage has been the deep, solid peace of a calm, composed spirit, resting in the embrace of Infinite Love. The breathing of my soul is, "The will of the Lord be done."

Do with me as seemeth thee good. Make me useful. Place me in circumstances as may best suit the purposes of thy grace for the attainment of this object. Only let me labor in thy vineyard, and choose thou the time and place.

I would gratefully record the blessing of God on an endeavor for the conversion of a soul last week — Miss B___. I went, by the request of our pastor, to visit her sister, who had experienced religion at the altar the day but one previous. Both Mrs. B___ and her sister were strangers to me; but after having received a satisfactory account from Mrs. B___ of her conversion, I turned to her sister and asked if she did not desire a like blessing.

"I do not know that I ever felt the need of it," she replied, in a very repulsive manner, and doubtless with the expectation of eluding all further attempts. Aware of the intention of her repulsive remarks and manner, and assured that she had been guilty of the awful sin of lying against the Holy Ghost, a holy boldness seemed to seize me, and, with yearning of heart, I began to set before her the awful nature of the sin she had just committed, by denying the work of the Spirit. "What," said I, "never felt yourself a sinner, in need of a Savior, when God hath said, that there is a light that enlighteneth every one that cometh into the world? It cannot be!" I felt that I was assisted by a power beyond myself, while endeavoring to persuade and warn her to flee the wrath to come.

It was thus I endeavored to sow the seed, and left the event with God. The next evening she went forward for the prayers of God's children, and last night she was brought most clearly into the light of his countenance. O my soul, magnify the Lord! My heart needed encouragement of this kind, in order to nerve it more firmly for future effort.

August 2. By faith ye stand. This is hourly verified in my experience; for were it by positive demonstration from any of the grosser senses, the eye of faith had ere this been closed, and my soul left in a state of darkness to be felt.

O! shall I ever lose this blessing which I have lately gained, and which I still by faith retain? this blessing for which I have so long struggled? My heart recoils at the thought yes, and my nature too, for it also partook of the living intensity with which it was sought. Blessed be God for ever, I feel that I need not lose it. My heavenly Father will not take it from me. He knows I could not answer the purpose for which his Son left his bosom in my behalf, without it.

That the enemy of all righteousness contends with me, is not matter of surprise. It would be were it otherwise. But O ! how much I need to be filled with the knowledge of the will of God, with all wisdom and spiritual understanding, in order to be better able to withstand, and also to understand the wiles of my foe!

I feel that I do grow in the knowledge of my Savior, though not so fast as my expectations have led me to desire. But my sufficiency is of thee, O Lord. I am thine — set apart — yes, sanctified to thy service; so say the breathings of my soul to my adorable Jesus.

Last night, the Lord my Redeemer condescended to take of the things of God and reveal them to me.

The enemy had been very powerfully suggesting throughout the day, and indeed much of the time since I received the blessing has been spent in struggling against the temptation, that *I believe just because I will believe.*

This suggestion assumed more plausibility during our afternoon meeting than at any other time. The beloved friends that attend this meeting, who have heard me so frequently speak of late of my earnest desires for this blessing, were waiting to rejoice in my joy, but so entirely by faith on the naked promises was I called to rely, that, were it not that I was fearful Satan might have a victory, did I not speak, I should have said nothing. Every moment while I was endeavoring to give in my testimony, the suggestion was urged, that I believed merely because I would believe. I now praise, the Lord that he enabled me to bear up amid this tempest, and give — just as I resolved in defiance of Satan I would do, a simple narration of the manner in which God brought me into the enjoyment of this blessing.

When he found he could not drive me from my purpose of making confession, he continuously urged upon me, while speaking, that the cold matter-of-fact manner in which I made my statements, as if destitute of all feeling, would prevent the reception of my testimony. How well that I had previously counted the cost — resolved to believe God at all hazards! I went to the evening meeting. Our dear brother S____ preached, but I scarcely heard a word. I had resolved to die ill the struggle to believe rather than to give up my confidence, and it seemed as if the matter had now come to a climax. I felt, after wrestling some time, that the Lord permitted me to come near the throne, and in much simplicity of heart, even as a little child to a tender parent, make known my grievances.

I said, O Lord, thou knowest that I would not believe merely because I will believe, without having a proper foundation for my faith. And now, in condescension to my constitutional infirmities, my proneness to reason, O give me this blessing in some such tangible form, that the enemy of my soul may never be successful with the temptation, that I believe merely because I will believe. Thou knowest that I would not believe, without a proper foundation for my faith; and now let me have this blessing in some such tangible form, that I may know the precise ground upon which I obtained, and also upon which I may retain it.

The answer came. New light burst upon my soul. The Holy Spirit took of the things of God, and revealed them unto me. It was by the unfolding of this passage to my understanding: "I beseech you, brethren, by the mercies of God, that ye present your bodies a living sacrifice, holy, acceptable, which is your reasonable service."

I now saw that I had *obtained* this blessing, by *laying all upon the altar.* I had *retained* it, by still *keeping* all upon the altar, "a *living* sacrifice." So long as it remained there, I perceived that both the faithfulness and the justice of

God stood pledged for its *acceptance*. While kept upon this altar, it *must* be cleansed from all unrighteousness, for the blood of Jesus *cleanseth;* not that it *can* or *will,* at some *future* period, *it cleanseth now, just when the offering is presented.*

By this I saw that I could no more *believe* for the *future* moment, than I could *breathe* for the future, and perceived that I must be contented to *live by the moment,* and rely upon God to sustain me in spiritual existence just as confidently as for sustainment in natural existence. So long as the offering was *kept upon the altar,* I saw it to be not only a privilege, but a *duty,* to believe.

I also saw that just so soon as I should begin to lean to my own understanding, feeling that I cannot do this or the other duty, just in the degree in which this is indulged in, the offering would be taken from off the altar, and I would have no *right to believe* the offering "holy and acceptable," inasmuch as it is not such an offering as God has declared acceptable by the voice of the written word.

The infinitely-efficacious blood was represented as ever flowing. And it is thus that the soul, laid upon the altar, is *cleansed* and kept *clean.*

O my soul, mayest thou ever remain upon the altar of sacrifice, and Thou, my strength and righteousness, forbid that any unhallowed act should ever cause its removal! It is by thy power alone, O God, that I am kept. Here shall I ever feel the cleansing efficacy. Here shall my soul fill and expand — fill and expand, till it shall burst its tenement, and faith shall be lost in sight.

August 6. My peace has not been so great yesterday and today. I see wherein I think I might have walked more carefully before God. I have lamented my short comings, and still feel that my all is upon the altar. I have resolved, through grace, to live in the most entire devotion to God. My inmost soul cries out, -

"None but Christ to me be given,
  None but Christ in earth or heaven."

Tomorrow, Providence permitting, I go to the grove, Hempstead Harbor, L. I. I have faith to believe that Jesus will go with me. My prayer is, "Unless thy presence go with me, send me not up." Lord, strengthen my own soul, and make me useful to others.

August 14. The Lord, my strength and righteousness, most gloriously answered the petition presented in that last written, even beyond my most enlarged expectations.

"He alone the work hath wrought."

Glory be to his name for ever. O how eminently near was the God of my salvation, while going to the grove, and through the whole progress of the meeting! I feel constrained to record to the glory of his grace, that he gave me a mouth to speak to others; to warn, entreat, and testify of his grace for the acceptance of all. He also gave me favor in the eyes of the people, and most truly did I experience that perfect love casteth out fear. I seemed to be borne quite above my natural timidity, my care being so fully cast upon Christ, the rock of my salvation.

I received a heartfelt assurance that the unction of the Holy One accompanied what I said to the hearts of others, and at times I was almost ready to stand still with amazement, and

"Wonder why such love to me;"

why the infinite God should so gloriously condescend to use an instrument so feeble. Well, it was all of grace; and I have thus without scarcely intending it (for I have surely been led in a way I knew not) assumed a character I ever wish to sustain — that of being zealous for the Lord of hosts. O! may my motto ever be, "Onward and upward," and God forbid that I should ever be less ardent in my course. My establishment in the blessing I have received has been more deep and thorough with the experience of each successive day. I have power continually to offer myself a *living* sacrifice, without any reserve, and feel that the blood of Jesus cleanseth from all unrighteousness.

In reference to my future course, I wish to lie passive in the hands of the Lord, as an instrument to perform his pleasure in all things. My will is lost in the will of God. I would not — dare not choose for myself though the choice were given. God is my all in all. I walk by faith, and am enabled to endure as seeing the Invisible, and my enjoyment consists in a calm, quiet resting on the promises of the gospel, assured that it is my Father's good pleasure to give me the kingdom. I feel at rest in the blessed persuasion, that if I, as a worker together with him, make use of the means ordained for my advancement thitherward, the point will be gained. *I know that the Holy Spirit has been given, the Comforter has come!* and has taken up his abiding residence in my heart — inciting me ceaselessly to every good word and work, and giving me a longing desire for the spiritual benefit of those around me — enabling me also to call upon God with a confidence heretofore unknown or unfelt, being assured that it is the principle of holy life within me, indicting my petitions and enabling me to exercise faith for the fulfillment of the promises. Glory be to the Triune God for such a salvation! I feel a holy ambition to lay up much treasure in heaven — to get near the throne.

One morning, during the progress of this meeting, I was blest in a very peculiar manner. I awoke about four o'clock, with an intense breathing after God. I felt assured by the manner in which my soul seemed to grasp a signal blessing that the Lord was about to seal me more fully his. My prayer was, Lord, *seal me unto the day of redemption*. There seemed to be a distinctiveness in the hallowed exercises of this season, that proclaimed the breathings of my heart to be the work of the Spirit, to a degree beyond any former occasion. For nearly two hours I remained under these peculiar influences, breathing forth in unutterable longings: "Lord, seal me, seal me unto the day of redemption." I was enabled to ask with such a degree of faith as to realize that I had the thing I desired of God. Though days have passed since, the assurance of the blessing then received has been increasing in stability. So sacred seemed the communion, so holy the covenant entered into between the everlasting God and the spirit that came forth from him, that I should be assimilated more and more to his own glorious image *here,* and be eventually reunited to him for ever, that I have not had one temptation to doubt. The work was so entirely of the Holy Spirit's operation on my heart, and such a sacred conviction of this possessed my mind, while passing through the exercises of that memorable morning, that even the tempter has been silent in this matter. Well may I sing, -

"My hope is full, O glorious hope
  Of immortality."

This was on Thursday, August the 10th. Surely it was a period to be remembered in the annals of eternity. Much of the day was spent in laboring for and with souls — persuading professors to the duty of deciding for God entirely, and encouraging them to enter by faith into the enjoyment of their already purchased inheritance.

I was also much engaged with some who were seeking to know a pardoning God. An interview with one of this description, a Mr.____ will long be remembered with peculiar pleasure. Such a genuine inquirer after truth, in whom such a vehement desire to know Christ was manifested, I have seldom witnessed. The Lord condescended to cause him to see the simple way of coming by faith, while I was conversing with him, and he soon began to repose in Christ as a *present* Savior. In endeavoring afterward to unfold to him the glory and extent of this salvation, he seemed to receive it with such ardor of feeling, and exhibited such maturity of views in the grasping of his desires, that I was constrained to offer, even for his acceptance, a full salvation: the extent to which he received it, remains to be determined by the fruits brought forth; but thus far (and I have minutely marked his progress) his Christian course has been signalized with an unusual degree of maturity and decision.

While we were dining this day, the table being loaded with the bounties of Heaven, I took advantage of the circumstance to expatiate on the fullness and freeness of the provision made by the gospel for all mankind — the ingratitude of man in refusing to partake of its proffered benefits, when by so many inducements invited.

Remembering that our beloved pastor had said, a few days since, that it was well to study human nature, and take advantage of its diversified peculiarities, I cast my eye on a stranger on the opposite side of the table, who looked as if whole-hearted in whatever he might undertake, and though an entire stranger, I felt as if I could read in his countenance, that he was whole-hearted in his rebellion against God. "Is it not *ungenerous,*" I asked, "when such bounteous provision has been made, and the great Master of the feast hath said, 'Come, for all things are ready,' that *any* should refuse?" "O," said he, "I do not think of these things as you do," and professed himself a Universalist. But I at once saw that I had touched upon the right chord in appealing to his ingratitude. An interesting conversation ensued, in which I felt the Lord touched his heart. I afterward took him upon my mind as a special subject of prayer. It was some time before he yielded to conviction, but on trying to extort a promise that he would pray for himself, in which I seemed to be unsuccessful, I said, "Well, if you will not pray for yourself, remember, there will be one praying for you between five and six every morning. God will hear and answer prayer; *I know it,* and though he will not irresistibly compel you to *yield* to the influences of his Spirit, he will irresistibly compel you to *feel* those influences; and if you resist them you will have to answer to God for the consequences." He was now moved in a manner I had not before witnessed, and though he did not promise to pray for himself, yet I perceived, by his embarrassed manner, that the Spirit was powerfully at work on his heart, giving him to see that he was hedged about, and placed in awfully-responsible circumstances. This was on board the steamboat returning home.

On the Sabbath succeeding I saw him, and his countenance bespoke that the rebellion of his heart had been, in a measure, subdued. "I have made up my mind," said he. But I afterward found that though his mind was made up mainly to devote himself to the service of God, there was one exception in which he determined to persist. *"I will never go forward to the altar for prayer,"* said he, *"God can just as well bless me anywhere else as there."*

I assured him, "that he would never find the Lord till he was willing to make any sacrifice, and to seek with all his heart." Fixed in his determination, he returned to his former state of rebellion, and, for a few weeks, continued sinning against the most awful convictions, until, at last, when just about to yield to the temptation to plunge into scenes of daring impiety, he concluded to take one more glance at the scenes of prayer to which he had of late accustomed himself, ere he made the plunge, when one of the Lord's dear servants, observing him at the door of the place of worship, put his arm round his neck and begged him to yield to Christ. He did yield; and scarcely had he knelt to declare himself an humble seeker of salvation, ere a mighty saving change passed over him, and I was soon afterward sent for to rejoice with him in the ardor of his first love.

He afterward informed me that at the time in the morning when I had said, *"Remember one will be praying for you,"* he had the most awful sense of his sinfulness, and the displeasure of God, and one morning, at this hour, his convictions rose to such a height that he arose and hid himself under the bed, as if to escape the presence of God. He is now apparently as wholehearted in the service of God as he was formerly in the service of Satan.

September 11. Precious Jesus,

"Where shall I thy praise begin?"

Thou hast not disappointed my expectations. More than my most sanguine hopes have been realized.

Yes! blessed be God, my course is still onward and upward. My communion is with the Triune God — my faith in his power and eternal veracity has been abundantly increased; I enjoy the constant visits of his love, and have realized that these visitations — nay, these abidings of his presence — are indeed transforming. Such has been the nearness of my communion, of late, that I have but to look up through the power of the Spirit and see Jesus at the right hand of the Father, pleading my cause; his inspiring language to my soul is, "Ask what thou wilt and it shall be done unto thee," and then it is but to make the request, in order to realize the immediate answer. Some answers to prayer, received of late, have indeed been extraordinary. Yes! I will sing, -

"Rise! rise, my soul! and onward, onward still,
        All is well, all is well,
God shall, with all, with all his fullness fill,
        All is well, all is well
Stronger than death his love to thee;
And thou to all eternity,
A monument of grace shalt be.
        All is well, all is well.

I was lately asked to converse with an irreligious young lady, when a suitable occasion might offer. The individual, on making the request, stated that the associations of the lady had been such, that much caution might be necessary in approaching her. I could not conceive much of an idea of a genteel neglecter of God, and felt rather disposed to indulge a disposition not to come in contact with her, thinking that I should give uneasiness to interested friends, should I declare what I believed to be the whole counsel of God to her soul, which I intended to do, should I fall in with her. Under unexpected circumstances, she was introduced, and I at once began to deliver what I believed to be a message from God to her soul.

The Lord condescended to make it at once a word in season; she became powerfully awakened, and the same day began to seek the Lord with all her heart, and the next morning was made a witness of his pardoning mercy.

She has since become as decided and ardent in the service of God as she formerly was in the service of the world — has become a witness of the perfect love of God, and is bringing forth fruit unto holiness.

September 9. Last evening, H____, the woman living with me, entered into the rest of perfect love. She had been struggling for it through the day with much fervor. Early in the evening she came to my room, and while conversing with her, the ardor of her desires so increased that she began to cry, "I will not let thee go until thou bless me." Her anguish was very great, so that her groans and cries might have been heard through the house.

The Lord whom she sought suddenly came to his temple, and his entrance was glorious. She was, for some time, quite overpowered with the weight of glory that rested upon her O! what am I, or my father's house before me, that I should be so favored of God? From her first coming to live with us, I have felt that the Lord sent her in answer to prayer. Assured that the most minute circumstances, inducing care, are not unknown to God, and as he hath said, For these things will I be inquired of by the house of Israel; I earnestly asked that he would take my cause in hand. It gave me much pleasure to hear her say, soon after she had been so powerfully blessed, "I asked the Lord to direct me to some place where I might enjoy Christian privileges, and, blessed be his name, this house has been a heaven to me ever since I came." Glory be to God!

After retiring to rest, I had severe buffetings from Satan. The conflict was so great that I awoke my dear companion to speak of it. He was so overcome with sleep that he scarcely aroused, but only said, "My grace is sufficient for thee." I immediately rose from my pillow, and renewedly, and yet more confidently, threw myself upon the all-sufficiency of grace — and, though the enemy did not cease to throw his darts, I trusted in my Savior to ward them off, and soon fell asleep; and awoke, after sweetly-refreshing repose, with peace reigning throughout all my borders, and filled with the joyous presence of God.

October 6. Still living in the enjoyment of a *present* salvation; my time has been so fully occupied of late, that I have not taken time to record the various loving kindnesses of the Lord as frequently as formerly; I have almost regretted this, for I ever prove it a blessing to be thus engaged, and then I find the review so inspiring for subsequent consideration.

I have been almost inclined to regard remissness in this, unless unavoidable, as remissness in duty. But the record is written upon my heart, and I trust, by the help of the Spirit, that the record of my daily walk and conversation may be a living epistle, read and known of all men, during my life; and in the world above tell for ever on the records of eternity, to the praise and glory of God.

God has, of late, in great mercy, made some of the young persons in my Bible class members of the household of faith; last Sabbath the excitement was so great, that we were not able to attend to the ordinary duties of the class; they are daily remembered by me before the Lord. *God is the hearer and answerer of prayer.*

I have also been permitted to see some gracious fruit of my labor on my tract district; several seem to have been, in a measure, awakened, while urging upon them the importance of religion. One, especially, a professed deist, possessed of talents of an order calculated to tell on the ranks of infidelity, has promised, and I believe sincerely, to investigate the truths of Christianity; my interest for him was much increased, by what human foresight would have pronounced an accidental circumstance. Part of my regular parcel of tracts for this month's distribution had been mislaid, and I took a few of the "Mother's Last Prayer" in my hand, in case the others should not hold out. From his knowledge of the subject of religion, I was impressed with the belief that he might once have had pious associations; I handed him the tract just mentioned, and said, "Perhaps you have had a pious mother?" he betrayed emotion, and said, "Yes." I now found the avenue to his heart much more accessible than before, and he acknowledged that he had been educated in Europe for the ministry in the Episcopal Church.

Other cases of much interest have come under my observation this month. Surely the work of tract distribution is the work of God; in no other duty do I feel more emphatically as a laborer in the vineyard. How noiselessly, and yet how effectually may the good seed here be sown, in hearts not otherwise accessible! Blessed be God that I was ever permitted to engage in this blessed cause!

Friday. A person of deep piety called in today, and in the narration of her early experience gave an unusual exhibition of the awful temerity of setting God a time. She is now about forty-three. At the age of fourteen, when away from home to attend school, God converted her soul. She continued very happy in the enjoyment of religion, and often thought with what great delight she would inform her friends, on her return home, of the happy change. One day, when on the eve of departure, as she was thinking wishfully of the scenes in which she was about to mingle, and of the surprise with which the gay circle would receive the intelligence of her conversion, she began to hesitate about the propriety of telling them at *once.*

The Spirit suggested, "You had better inform them immediately, or you may never do it." The tempter presented, in glowing exhibition, the disappointment of gay young friends, who would regard her as for ever lost to their society, should she profess her conversion. The Spirit of God strove mightily; but notwithstanding she had been favored with much of its happying influences, so strong were the world's delusive phantoms, that she deliberately made up her mind, after thinking of it some time, not to say anything on the subject of religion: and in doing this the Spirit assured her that she would in effect give up the subject entirely. Awful to relate, she concluded to let the matter come to this point, and resolved to give up the enjoyment of religion altogether, until she should arrive at the age of twenty. The Spirit of God from that moment ceased its strivings, and she was left to pursue, unchidden, the follies of the world.

When about eighteen she was arrested by a very singular disease. Many physicians were consulted, but her case was pronounced inexplicable. It began with a slight malconformation of her person, which gradually increased to such a degree, as at first to embitter, and eventually forbid all enjoyment in the gay scenes to which she had been most ardently devoted. She now saw, and Satan seemed also to love to taunt her with, the barter she had made, and for a time she was left to reflect on her folly in utter despair of the mercy of God. She imagined that she had received the mark of Cain, and was unwilling to look up to either God or man. Her person continues to be increasingly deformed. But some years since, after a long season of despair, she was enabled to trust in the mercy of God, and is now a happy believer; yet still fully believes that she carries about in her person the mark of the displeasure of the Almighty.

October. Went to the tract distributors' meeting this evening. Had a very delightful and profitable season. I was much drawn out in prayer that every soul might be blest. The divine sanction seemed to be given, and a heavenly influence appeared to pervade the minds of all present, while in sweetest unity those of different denominations joined together in humble effort and aspirations for the success of this blessed cause. Surely it has most peculiarly the smiles of our Lord.

November 20. The Lord still condescends to water the seed sown in my Bible class. Three more profess to have found the Lord. I dare not doubt the genuineness of the change. The Savior said, "By their fruits ye shall know them," and they manifest most obviously that the love of God is shed abroad in their hearts, by their ardent love and zeal for the salvation of others. There seems to be a general awakening in the class. The Lord has laid the burden of their souls upon me in such a manner, that my soul is continually saying, "I will not let thee go" until thou bless them. O what a stewardship, to have souls in charge!

November 27. Called today on some Christian friends. I was greatly interested with one young friend just on the verge of eternity. She is young and fascinating: but just merged into womanhood, and life opening with exhilaration before her. Yet the opening prospects of life and immortality possess still greater charms, as the world recedes from her vision and the expectation of recovery decreases. She is now longing to go, and her cry is, "Lord, give me patience to wait thy time." I have thought that the Lord was taking her from the evil to come. But a few months since, in the midst of an excitement in religion, she was taken into the fold of Christ. A renunciation of gay society and conformity to the world seemed not to have been included in the account, when she espoused the cause of Christ. Some Christian friends, who had counted the cost, knew well that a life of piety, founded on such principles, could not endure the storms of temptation to which she stood continually exposed, by the associations surrounding her, and tremblingly they watched her progress. But the heavenly Watcher, almighty in power and infinite in love, is now about taking her most gently from the impending storm.

From a review of the circumstances in which this young lady was placed, my mind has been much impressed with the weight of responsibility resting upon those parents, who, though they have embraced religion with its self-denying principles, as the better way for themselves, yet, as though the children with which God hath intrusted them were in a manner distinct from themselves, bring them up and place them in associations calculated to fascinate them with the frivolities which they have renounced, as inconsistent with a life of piety. How strange the infatuation! It is in effect bringing them up in a way from which they intend and pray that they should depart, while they encourage the pursuit.

December 5. While at meeting last evening, a new and singular source of temptation was presented, and God gave me a signal victory. The Lord has of late permitted the fruit of my labor to be apparent to an unusual degree. "You would not labor so assiduously," said the tempter, "were it not that the fruits were evident to those around you." Seldom have I felt more indignant, and I began to anticipate, with a longing to which I had almost been a stranger, a speedy dismission from the body, so that my free spirit, unvexed by the accusations of Satan, might soar unhindered on any errand of love to which God might appoint. Yes, I began to long for the freedom of a disembodied spirit, where, unobserved by mortals, I might do the will of God as angels do in heaven. At once a sphere of labor was presented, where, unobserved by any other than the eye of God, I might work. The minister who was preaching was a timid young brother, and there were elder brethren in the ministry listening, which seemed to weigh heavily upon his spirit.

It was suggested, You may help that young brother by asking in faith, that the Spirit may help his infirmities, and speak through him. The Lord now gave a perfect victory over Satan, by inspiring my soul with mighty faith in pleading for his servant. And God did indeed speak through him. The brother seemed raised above his former self, and though not previously a tine of awakening in our church, several souls were powerfully awakened through the exercises of the meeting. Ten went forward to be prayed for. Never before had I such a view of the impotency of human instruments. Not only did I know, but I felt, beyond the power of expression, that they were powerless, only as God condescended to give them efficiency. After the persons had presented themselves for prayer, it was suggested, This may all amount to nothing after all this ado; it is sudden excitement, which will not be likely to eventuate in much. I then began to plead that every one of them might be converted before leaving the altar, and at the close of the meeting the announcement was made that every one of them had been blest.

Dec. 13. All the ardent desires of my soul are sweetly centered in God. I feel that I have not one desire apart from that which may promote his glory. He is my all in all. I enjoy a silent heaven of love. The beauty of holiness more and more captivates my enraptured soul. Spirit of holiness, continue to breathe upon me thy purifying, soul-transforming influences! I have ever found, after every season of intense wrestling for more conformity to the divine image, that it has invariably been given, though I may not at the time have realized it. We cannot draw nigh to God without proving that he draws nigh to us, though at the moment our faith may be tried, and we not fully apprehend it. Communion with God must necessarily be transforming.

Dec. 14. At our class meeting, last night, God was eminently present. The place seemed to be sensibly filled with the divine presence. Mrs.___ was present, and gave in a glowing testimony. About three months since she was translated from the kingdom of darkness to the kingdom of God's dear Son, through the instrumentality of a devoted female friend. Previous to this her associations were with the gayest of the gay. Theaters, ball rooms, and parties were the life of her existence. But, O, what a transformation grace hath made! From her first setting out, she gave up the world, and became wholehearted in the service of God. It was on the next day after her conversion that the Spirit assured her she must leave the things which were behind, and urge her way onward to the attainment of holiness. Two weeks since she obtained the blessing. It was not hard to get at the meaning of being sanctified throughout, body, soul, and spirit, while beholding her enraptured countenance last night. Her very looks carried a conviction to the heart, that she was filled with the sanctifying influences of the Spirit. Since her conversion, her husband, mother, and servant, with two or three other members of the family, have all sought and found the Lord,. How striking the difference in the progress of Mrs.___ and the majority of those who set out in the heavenly way, too many of whom seem neither to have counted the cost, nor to have made calculation on the sacrifice of *all* things for Christ! And how many of such seem to be a hindrance to their unconverted friends, by holding out a false light, rather than agents to bring them, by persuasive example and mighty prayer, to that Savior who hath said, "Except a man take up his cross and follow after me, he cannot be my disciple!"

Jan. 4. I have been praying of late for power to apprehend more fully the hope of my calling. I have longed for clearer perceptions of the glory of my inheritance. The desire of my heart has been granted. Heaven seems not only near, but as in part enjoyed. Yes, eternal life is begun. The presence of God fills my soul, and

"His presence makes my paradise,
And where he is, is heaven."

I have sometimes thought that the enjoyments of glorified spirits in heaven, and of those possessing the full salvation of the redeemed on earth, differ mainly in degree and not in nature. An aged brother, who seems to be on the borders of the promised land, gave an interesting relation, last night, of one lately escaped from earth. He was standing by her bedside at the eve of her departure. "Do you hear the angels sing?" said she.

The individual addressed said, "No, I do not. Do you?"

"Yes," she replied, "I do."

"And why cannot you join with them?" inquired the friend.

She then began, and, in tones and words of unearthly sweetness, joined, as was fully believed by the surrounding company, with the heavenly choristers. "I never heard the like before," said the aged saint, "and I never expect to hear it again this side of heaven." The physician, an unconverted man, standing by, was filled with astonishment, and said, "I would not have missed that for a hundred dollars."

Jan. 31. My faith has been both tried and strengthened by a circumstance of recent occurrence. It being necessary for me to change a servant, I confidently sought direction from God in making the exchange. I almost immediately found that she was in no ordinary degree a servant of the wicked one. I never remember to have had one about me that seemed more truly under demoniacal influence. I thought her unhappiness seemed in part to arise from the fact that she could not, by her various provocations, disturb the heavenly quietness of those around her. I would have parted with her immediately, but thought I would keep her one week, solely for the purpose of seeing whether Almighty grace might not, in some way, subdue her heart. The last day of trial came, and matters seemed to have grown worse instead of better. As I knelt before the Lord in order to present her case, and also to implore divine direction in filling up her place, the enemy suggested, Did you not believe yourself to have been directed in getting the one you are now about to part with? and behold, it has been evil and only evil, and that continually! Is this not enough to make you question whether God regards all these little matters? The suggestion indeed seemed plausible, but my heart said, "Though I die, I will not remove my integrity from me." And I concluded the matter thus: Perhaps after she has been weeks or months from us, she may remember that there was something in religion to make people happy, and to sustain them under provocations; something she has heard may be as seed sown, which may result in her conversion months hence. As I rose from committing my cause believingly to God, I was called into another room to converse with a penitent greatly distressed. He remained two or three hours, his agony apparently continually increasing. In the mean time the woman came repeatedly to the door to call us to dine, and I as often beckoned her away, as I had no intention of leaving him until he had received comfort. A shade of uneasiness crossed my mind as she looked in on his distress lest she might form strange ideas of religion on witnessing such violent emotions of sorrow; but I cast my care upon God, assured of his ability to take care of his own work, and continued to point him to the Savior, and to wrestle in prayer with him until deliverance came. The transition was glorious and almost overwhelming. In the mean time, my dear husband, with others, had come in, and the now happy child of God, almost beside himself with joy, went hastily around the room, grasping the hand of each, with flowing tears, exclaiming, "O, bless the Lord He has forgiven all my sins. O, bless the Lord — bless the Lord !" At this crisis the woman again came to the parlor door to repeat the call for dinner. Seeing the door open, he ran to it in his bewilderment of joy, and, grasping her hand, exclaimed, "O, praise the Lord! He has forgiven me all my sins. O, praise the Lord!" He continued these exclamations, still holding her hand, while tears of joy coursed down his cheeks most rapidly. The fact that no responsive feeling answered to his joy, seemed only to prolong his appeal, and he continued to retain her hand, still exclaiming, "O, praise the Lord!" A few minutes after we went to dine, when, to the rejoicing of our hearts, we witnessed that God had at last touched her stony heart. She had been weeping bitterly, and hastened, on seeing us, to another room, to hide her emotion. Afterward, on conversing with her, I found that she was most powerfully awakened. On trying to encourage her to seek the Lord, "O!" said she, "I shall never reach that ark of safety. I had a dream some time since, when I saw an ark floating down a river, and it was said to me, 'You will never reach that ark of safety.'" She continued in great distress until time for evening meeting. It was necessary for me to remain at home if she went, and I advised her to improve the first moment of opportunity that was given for seekers to present themselves for prayer. I afterward learned from one who saw her, that just so soon as the invitation was given, she literally rushed forward, as if driven to desperation by a consciousness that her case would admit of no delay. When there, with an impetuosity of feeling, which could only arise from the view she afterward told me she had of the impending wrath of God, that seemed to be resting down upon her soul, in such fearful magnitude, that she felt as if life could not have been sustained any longer, unless it had been removed, she cried, "God have mercy upon me;" and she continued to cry, as did Bartimeus, with a loud voice, "God have mercy on me, a sinner," and like him, strange to relate, she was chidden by some of the Lord's well-meaning children. But they knew not the anguish of her spirit. Toward the close of the exercises I was released from home, and went to the meeting. The cry, "Lord have mercy," met my ear as I entered, but though I knew all things were possible with God, I could scarcely conceive that the pride of C__y had been so suddenly put down as to bring her to that point. But on ascertaining that it was indeed she, I hastened to the altar. On being apprised that I was coming, she turned toward me, and, with one of the most imploring looks I ever witnessed, exclaimed, "O! my dear Mrs.___, do you think God can have mercy upon me?" She seemed to be, in a measure, soothed, while, with sympathetic feelings, I endeavored to point her to the Lamb of God. She continued to cling to the altar, though the people had mostly retired, until God spoke peace to her soul. But her case, after conversion, was strikingly dissimilar from the one in the morning, or unlike any that I have before witnessed. After she was forgiven she seemed to be so overwhelmed with the stupendous mercy of God, that I do not remember that she uttered a syllable expressive of joy. We knew that Jesus in a moment bade the troubled waves be still, by the sudden stillness that succeeded. There was a great calm; but the solemnity of death sat on her countenance, and she now willingly, and, I think, silently rose and left the altar. The next day she informed me that, on retiring to rest that night, she tried to pray, but scarcely knew how. It was a duty to which she had been a stranger. In the morning she arose about four o'clock, and "O!" she exclaimed, "I could pray then."

About ten, on the morning of the same day, while arranging matters in the room where I was sitting, the person who had been instrumental in bringing her to the house came in, and she went down to see her. "Did you tell Emma what God has done for your soul?" I inquired.

"O yes," she replied, "I feel as if I wanted to tell all the world."

"I am glad you do feel so, C___," said I, "for I should be inclined to think, that one not desirous to spread such good news had deceived herself."

It was probably the first time she had ever heard it possible for persons to deceive themselves in matters of religion, and Satan took the advantage of her ignorance in a moment. She dropped the work on which she was engaged, and, as if astounded, exclaimed, "Am I *deceived*?"

"No, C___," said I, "you are not deceived; it is the enemy of your soul who tells you so; you are no more deceived than I am." The contest lasted for a few moments, and it really seemed as if she would have given up her confidence, and have lost all, when all at once, just as suddenly as the tempter had come, he was driven away, and, strange to relate, she threw herself on her knees at my feet, and began to exclaim in a transport of joy, "*No, I am not deceived!* I am not deceived! Mrs. ___, your *prayers* have saved me. Her joy was now as ecstatic and communicative, as was that of the individual who the day before had been instrumental in her awakening.

I have learned lessons through these circumstances, which I trust ever to remember. One is, never to give way to discouragement, however dark and contradictory intervening providences may appear. Another, that the Lord has his *own* way of doing his *own* work. His thoughts are not as our thoughts. I thought the extreme distress of Mr.___ prejudicial to the interest of religion in the mind of the wicked C___. From her distress, I also became convinced that it is in mercy to the guilty soul that the Almighty withholds a full view of the exceeding sinfulness of sin, as it would doubtless paralyze its energies, and it would sink, overwhelmed with the view, into the horrors of an awful eternity. And yet another lesson, and I think it indeed important. I might have been a partaker in the over-solicitude of those dear friends, who "charged her to hold her peace," had I not been personally acquainted with the circumstances of the case, and known with what perfect aversion she would have regarded the circumstance of making such a spectacle of herself, had it not been for those overwhelming perceptions of guilt, which doubtless swallowed up every thought of outward things. We, had thought ourselves on the eve of a glorious revival, but since that night a check, sudden and mysterious, has been put to the work. The change was so sudden, that some have said, "Sister, what do you think can be the cause?" My mind has invariably attributed it to one cause, and that is, that the ark of God was over-solicitously steadied, when that individual was urged to hold her peace, and when it was said, "What a pity that the meeting should have been so disturbed, when it was only ___'s servant!"

At the commencement of this protracted meeting, I was very desirous that a day of fasting and prayer should be observed by our people for its success. I hardly know why it was, but the suggestion did not receive official sanction to the degree anticipated. I concluded to observe the day previous to the commencement of the meeting thus, to the degree that my infirm health would allow, and I have not only been much blessed and strengthened in my own soul, but the Lord has condescended to bless my endeavors to be useful to others, beyond what has been ordinary with me on similar occasions. Several seekers have found the Lord while at our house.

March 14. On Monday evening, at the Sabbath school prayer meeting, an opportunity was offered for speaking, which, on ordinary occasions, I had been accustomed to improve. Seldom have I been required to walk more exclusively by naked faith, contending against the buffetings of the enemy. A short silence ensued, and no one seemed ready to fill up the time. A new trial presented. I did not seem to have one word to say; — barrenness in reference to the subject, and conflicts with the enemy, would have prevented my saying anything, had it not been said to my soul, "Now is the time to test the faithfulness of God; he hath said, 'Open thy mouth wide, and I will fill it.' If you do not speak now that the circumstances require it, it will be said, 'What do ye more than others?" and now, if you would prove his faithfulness, you must open your mouth *first,* and then *trust to God to fill it.* Upon the strength of the promise I arose. God did fill my mouth in such a manner as it had never been filled before on a similar occasion. Blessed liberty of soul was at once given, every snare broken, and my soul rejoiced with a joy unspeakable and full of glory. Soon as the exercise demanding the effort had passed over, the trial of my faith was again resumed, and continued, until it seemed necessary, from the circumstances in which I was placed, that I should join in prayer. I commenced with feelings similar to those under which I had spoken, and God again gave blessed liberty. Yesterday, at our afternoon meeting, my exercises, and the trial of my faith, were identical with those of the evening previous, and the grace to help in time of *need* was bestowed *when* required, and withdrawn when *not* required, precisely as it had been on Monday evening. Well, let it be even so. I have counted the cost of living a life of *faith* on the Son of God, and now that I am brought to the test, shall I repine?

March 29. The Lord has brought my soul into a place of broad rivers. Rivers, as they verge toward the mighty ocean, become broader and deeper. Thus I find in my onward course, the nearer I approach the ocean of infinite purity, love, and unbounded blessedness, the more my soul partakes of the nature of those enjoyments, and becomes yet more closely and consciously allied to the glorious source to which it is tending.

My faith has been strengthened, and my soul much blessed, in reading an account of the Christian experience and happy death of a little sufferer, who has lately finished her pilgrimage at the age of nine. She was an extraordinary sufferer, with a spinal affection, for about two years before her death.

Her friends cannot remember to have heard one murmuring or repining word during the whole progress of her illness. She gave a uniform exhibition of the blessed overflowings of a heart where

"Christ alone did dwell,
All praise, all meekness, and all love."

She was subject to the most violent paroxysms of pain, yet when asked, "Would you not like to get well?" would reply, "No; I do not think it is the will of God, therefore I would not." Her experience brought out to an unusual degree the meaning of the Savior's words, "Except ye become as little children," &c. It is said that she regarded the Bible as *literally* the *word of God*, and treasured it up in her heart, with all that childlike simplicity and sweetness that it might have been supposed she would have done had the Savior spoken audibly to her.

April 6. I have been reading a book entitled, "The Importance of Small Things." The author (a good man, I am sure) differs greatly in opinion from the generality of professors of the present day. I should suppose that truth lies between the two. It is my opinion that the Lord generally calls us to be lights to those around us, by a consistent Christian example, in just the circle from which he has singled us out. Those of" Cesar's household" were possessed of an influence, from social causes, to be useful to those of the king's palace, above others who were unaccustomed to scenes of loyalty, and its various unenviable associations; but yet it should not be forgotten that there were saints even there. And thus with those of every grade in life. God makes use of our moral and social training in fitting us for the place in his temple which he designs we should fill. Placed there by his own hand, we adorn and beautify it; elsewhere, we deform it by evident unseemliness. Paul speaks of being all things to all men, in order by any means to win some. And Christ also says, "The children of this world are wiser in their generation than the children of light." This was doubtless in allusion to their various nameless expedients to advance their worldly interests. As illustrative of this, one brother remarked, some time since, that if he was among the Indians, and could do more good by wearing a blanket, he would wear one. This recognizes, in my opinion, the principle upon which Paul practiced; a principle which the Lord deeply implanted in my soul, the hour when he gave me the witness of perfect love. I have felt since that I have no interest apart from the interests of the Redeemer's kingdom. The Lord has assured my soul that the kingdom of heaven does not consist in meats and drinks, but in righteousness, peace, and joy in the Holy Ghost. Yet, O! how I have mourned to witness some, who, from a love of conformity to the world, feed the vanity of the unsanctified heart, prove a stumbling block in the way of others, and make shipwreck of faith and a good conscience. Some, doubtless, will find in the eternal world, that the priceless soul has been lost, through the valueless trifles of mere outward adornment. Not that there was sin in the articles themselves, but in the pride which they tended to cherish. Yet these are nice points to determine. I have known some inclined to unchristianize those who did not conform to a standard which had perhaps been begotten from early parental prejudices and associations. I have seen others also who seemed influenced by the principle, that unlovely habits, and manners uncouth, were necessary to mortify the pride of the heart; and that the exhibition of these unlovely traits is needful, in order to show that the heart is humble: such do not appear to be aware that they are in the meantime sinning against the express Scriptural requirements, "Be courteous," "Whatsoever things are lovely," &c. It seems very reasonable to me that the Christian, whom Christ hath chosen out of the world, should manifest in spirit, manner, and dress, a detachment from the things of earth.

April 17. I have found blessed satisfaction late in bringing the promises and the Promiser together. What a privilege to be permitted to take God on the strong ground of his own infallible word!

I called today to see H___, the woman who was so greatly blessed, while living with us, some time since. She has been sick several weeks, and is apparently just on the verge of heaven. On asking her whether she would not rather depart and be with Christ, she replied, "If raising my finger would decide the point, I would not dare to do it."

Her health had become so infirm that it was necessary she should embrace an opportunity, which offered, of living where she would have but little to attend to. On going there, she found that the family in which she had engaged did not have family prayer, the husband being irreligious. H___ expressed her disappointment, and said she felt as if she could not stay in a family where she should be deprived of this privilege. She then modestly said to the lady, who was a Christian woman;" If Mrs. ____ will pray and read one morning, I will the next." The lady consented to the proposal. The husband soon began to manifest interest on the subject of religion, and the Lord laid the weight of his soul on H___'s mind in such a manner, that, to use her own language, she reeled as one intoxicated, under the weight of her feelings. This intense excitement was more especially felt during one Sabbath. As she was going to church, she was so absorbed in travail of soul for him that she was forgetful of all around her, or where she was, and being unable to proceed to church, she sat down by the way, and continued, she was not aware how long, in agony of soul for him. That night he went to the inquiry room, became deeply awakened, and soon afterward became a happy believer in Christ; and in heaven will doubtless remember the humble individual who was instrumental in rearing the family altar.

July 2. O, what a heavenly sweetness has just been diffused throughout my soul! I took up a book and read these lines

"I dwell for ever on His heart,
 For ever he on mine."

Yes, Jesus loves me. I know it — I feel it. What can I want besides? O, may I ever be consciously and constantly filled with the Spirit!

July 9. The weather of late has been very oppressive, and my health infirm. Last night, on retiring, I felt the spirit willing, but the flesh weak. During the hours of sleep, Satan seemed to be chiding me with a want of energy, when the word of the Lord was applied with such power and sweetness to my mind, that it awoke me. "He that keepeth Israel, neither slumbereth nor sleepeth." I rejoiced and gave thanks to the God of my salvation.

David says, "At midnight I will arise and give thanks unto thee, because of thy righteous judgments." Psalm cxix, 62. I have found it very profitable to follow his example. O! with what nearness of access have I been permitted to approach the throne at this hallowed hour! At times it seems as if faith had almost turned to sight.

August. Have met with some friends on the heavenly way of late, in whom I have been much interested, especially at our recent camp meeting. One, the Rev. Mr. M___, pastor of a Congregational Church, I shall doubtless ever remember from the manner in which the Lord made him instrumental in communicating a lesson, which has been rendered a great blessing to me. I met him first on the morning of the day, at a social meeting in one of the tents, where Jesus was eminently present. He spoke with such power and sweetness of the deep things of God, as conveyed a conviction to the hearts of the friends of Jesus, that the secret of the Lord was with him. I was also greatly blessed in my own soul, and was permitted to feel sweet freedom of spirit, while conversing on the things of God. After the meeting closed, we were introduced, and permitted to take sweet counsel together.. This was previous to the morning exercises from the stand. At noon, he came to our tent, and to my surprise and sorrow saluted me thus: "Well, Mrs. ___, if I should be saying something very good about you, I should be praising you should I not?" Contemplating a religious compliment, which I most conscientiously disapprove, and disappointed that I had, as I conceived, made miscalculations in reference to the depth of his knowledge in the things of God, I looked up at him reprovingly, and with evident displeasure said, "I suppose it would be called so." He hesitated a moment, long enough to let me form enduring conceptions of the trial, and then, with childlike sweetness, said, "Let us speak good of God." Then turning to the company, with a beseeching look and tone, he added, "Come, let us all speak well of the name of the Lord. He has done much for us. *He* will not be offended, for he hath said, 'Whoso offereth *praise, glorifieth me.*'" Many Scriptural exhortations to *praise* the Lord were then brought forward, and we had a blessed season in speaking well of the name of the Lord. I have not been perplexed in any degree with the temptation since, that I am talking about *myself,* when I am telling what the *Lord has done for me.* I feel that praising the Lord is by far the most effectual way of disclaiming the work, which some, untaught in the things of God, might conceive to be inherent good in the creature; and I have since felt and cherished an increased longing to communicate, to the *praise of God*, the work of his Spirit on my heart. The proper principle of *humility* has thus, by this trial, been brought with such tangibility within my grasp, as to leave a continual and blessed certainty on my mind, that God has indeed given me the grace of perfect humility. I joyfully acknowledge it, to the glory of his grace. If God has given it, it is *his gift. I* have not *given it to myself.* O, how much I love to praise his name! Well may the poet say,

"— Eternity's too short
To utter all His praise."

God gave me a signal answer to prayer also on the morning of this memorable day. My heart had been earnestly aspiring after greater conformity to the Divine Image, and stronger faith, during the preceding day. The last breathing, as I fell asleep at night was, "Lord increase my faith." I was awakened in the morning, at a very early hour, by the powerful application of this passage, "And this is the confidence that we have in him, that if we ask anything according to his will, he heareth us; and if we know that he hear us, whatsoever we ask, we know that we have the petitions that we desired of him." The Holy Spirit took of the things of God and revealed them to me, and I received clearer and more inspiring views of the simplicity of faith than ever before.

At the previous morning meeting alluded to, while the disciples of Jesus were talking so sweetly of the things that appertain to the kingdom, my mind for a few moments was drawn from the interesting circle to my beloved companion, who, by professional duties, was seldom permitted to participate in such scenes. Gratitude, desire, and sympathy blended, in contrasting the amount of my privileges with his. "O how much he would enjoy such a season as this," thought I; when this question was presented to me, "Why may he not be especially and powerfully blest *just* now, where he is?"

"All human probabilities are against it," was suggested in reply; "he is *just now* riding about the streets of a busy city, and it would be out of the ordinary way of God's manner of working, and he does not work miracles when his ordinary way of dealing may just as well be submitted to." Immediately the truth was presented, that all things are possible with God, and all things are possible to him that believeth. Is it not according to the will of God that he should be blest now? Does not the whole spirit of his word warrant you in this belief? And if it is according to his revealed will, then you have the confidence that he heareth you and if you know that he *heareth,* then you may *know* that you *have* the things you desire of him. I now felt that I had a sufficient warrant from the word, to assure me that I might ask confidently; and I began to say, "O, Lord! distance, time, and place are one with thee — O, bless him — bless him just now in a powerful manner, wherever he may be. I leave my petition before the throne, presented in the name of Jesus." I felt a perfect confidence that what I had asked was according to the will of God, and knew that I had the things I had desired of God. My mind was then recalled to the circumstances by which I was surrounded. The answer to my petition was not again brought to my recollection until the Sabbath after my return, when my husband remarked what a blessed day he had on Thursday. "All at once," said he, "as I was riding about, with my mind in no way specially engaged, such a heavenly influence came down upon me, and remained with me all day, that I thought some one must have been praying for me. Was it not you?" I then told him the manner in which I had been engaged that morning, and the answer received, and we had a season of rejoicing together, in view of the condescension of God.

August. Met another traveler in the highway today. He gave a statement of the manner of the Spirit's operations, which, though unusual, was instructive and edifying. How truly, in reference to the work of the Spirit, may it be said, "There are diversities of operations, but it. is the same God which worketh all in all!" And yet in the early career of the believer, how anxious he generally is to get an experience in minutiae, like others, and how prone to dissatisfaction when this is not attained! Mr. ___ received his early training with the Hicksite Friends. His prepossessions, as may be presumed, were all opposed to excitement in religion. The Lord gave him a pious wife, who, in process of time, became a traveler in the way of holiness. In the meanwhile, when pleading with God in his chamber, he was also made a partaker of the pardoning mercy of God, and united in church fellowship with his companion. He was glad when she became a zealous seeker of holiness, hoping that her experience might be instructive to him, as he knew but little about the subject, otherwise than as he had heard of it merely as a doctrine peculiar to a sect. One Sabbath afternoon, while sitting in the house of the Lord, in an unexpected moment, apart seemingly from any human instrumentality, light — in reference to the nature of the blessing, and the terms upon which it was to be received — was presented in a luminous manner, for his acceptance The terms on his part were, the entire sacrifice of all to God, and the taking upon himself the obligation to profess the blessing on receiving it. He remembered some who were over him in the Lord, who did not profess holiness, and. thought, "Surely they will not receive my testimony, and will think me assuming, or presumptuous;" and though he much desired the blessing, he finally concluded that he would not at once make up his mind to receive it on such terms. On coming to this conclusion, the light he had received in reference to the nature of the blessing, and the manner in which it was offered for his acceptance, and all prospect of attaining it, vanished as suddenly as it had been presented. For the two succeeding months, darkness to be felt brooded over his pathway. In apparently-unavailing lamentations, he bemoaned his refusal to comply with the conditions, scarcely daring to hope that the Spirit would again take of the things of God, and reveal them to him. But suddenly, as on the former occasion, while under the word, the blessing was again offered, and the same conditions were presented.. With eagerness, his whole heart flew to embrace the offer, and said, "Let it come in any way, only let it come!"

It came, and with such mighty power, that the day of Pentecost could scarcely have witnessed, in individual experience, a scene more astounding, uncontrollable, or unaccountable, on the principles of mere human reason, than was presented in his extraordinary exercises. The "sound from heaven, as of a rushing mighty wind," could scarcely have been more overwhelming in its influences on that day, when anciently given, than on this occasion.

For about four hours he was no more under his own control, or that of his friends around him, than the apostles were when first baptized with the Holy Ghost. Many others were baptized as suddenly at the same time. He still continues a flaming witness of the power of saving grace.

Wednesday. I was much blessed today by a remark from Dr. Bangs. "We lose much," said he, "in not being *definite* in our petitions. Now what do we most want? — let that be at the present time the definite subject of our petitions." I began to ask myself, "What do I most want?" I remembered that Jesus had said, "Whatsoever ye shall ask the Father, in my name, he will give it you." I asked for an enlargement of soul, and then that these enlarged capacities might be filled with God. I left my petition before the throne, in the name of Jesus; but felt assured that I should have the things I had desired of God. Almost immediately after I was requested to converse with one earnestly seeking the Lord. Soon afterward, at an unexpected moment, I found surprising expansion of soul, and was filled with the fullness of God to such a degree, that I was led to exclaim, "What can this mean?" when a conviction, as powerful as though audibly uttered, assured me, "This is the answer to the petition that you some time since left before the throne, in the name of Jesus."

Thursday. Learned a lesson today. The manner of learning it was somewhat painful. The Lord grant that the effect may be lasting. "He doth not afflict the children of men *willingly*." O' that I may not grieve the heart of Infinite Love, by making it needful, by my thoughtlessness, for him to repeat the lessons intended to be communicated through each trial, as I pass onward in the heavenly way. I was constantly so surrounded by the multitude, that I began to long most ardently for opportunity to get into the secret presence of the Lord. I had for the few days preceding been endeavoring to bear the burdens of others with but little intermission, and had thus far been permitted but little time for the purpose of presenting my own case before the Lord. Now, thought I, I *will get alone with God*. Am I to presume that this ability to be useful will last, if I thus permit my seasons for private devotion to be broken in upon by these ceaseless interruptions? Finding, if I remained in the tent, there was but little prospect of obtaining my wish, I concluded to seek some solitary place apart from the multitude; but turn which way I would, I met with some one disposed to beguile my time. At last, despairing to obtain it thus, I turned, with resolve not to be foiled, to my tent, determined that I would have it there. Scarcely had I retired with the intention of trying to feel alone, though still but little removed from the multitude, when dear sister S____ said," Sister, Mrs. G____ wishes to see you." I looked up with a degree of disappointment, and said, "O, dear!" and went to see the friend. She had come purposely to seek advice in reference to the way of holiness; but I found that I had not the special help of the Spirit in conversation which I had been accustomed to enjoy, and was startled at the difference. The ability to be useful seemed to be withheld. It was then apprehended, most keenly, that the ability was a special gift from God. On inquiring of the Lord, after the friend had retired, why it was that this trial was permitted, I was immediately given to see that I had been endeavoring, though ignorantly, to get out of the order of God. And I now see that the only way to be a blessing to others, or to be blessed, is by entering promptly and rejoicingly into the providential openings thus hourly presented, and that the time to work is plainly indicated by the manner of the Spirit's operations on the hearts of others in sending them to me; and such labor is as truly the work of the Lord, and as pleasing to him, as is the devotion of the closet. It was not a willful trespass. My heavenly Father knew it, and did not severely chide; but he taught me a lesson which I hope ever to profit by when similarly circumstanced. O, how much need for the continual application of the blood of Jesus! Under the old dispensation, atonement was necessary for sins of ignorance. Under the new, a High Priest who can be touched with the feelings of our infirmities ever presents the soul-cleansing, peace-speaking blood in our behalf, and the sacrifice still ascends, a sweet savor of Christ, unto God. It was said by one, "Conviction is net condemnation." How important, for the peace of the soul, is this knowledge! In the experience just narrated, I have proved the justness of the remark. Willful transgression necessarily brings condemnation; but a kind father may convict a dutiful child of unintentional error, and yet not condemn him.

Sunday. I was permitted to partake of the precious memorials of the Savior's dying love, and was enabled, through the blood of the everlasting covenant, to enter into closer and more sensible communion with God than I can express. While bringing to lively remembrance the momentous price paid for the redemption of the soul, and summing up every power and faculty, that nothing might be wanting to make the sacrifice complete, I realized, most deeply and consciously, that I was enabled to lay hold upon the strength of Omnipotence, and enter into covenant with the Lord my Redeemer. Such a full and delightful assurance was given that I had, through the Spirit, complied with the terms of the covenant, and had given all, and was now receiving all in Christ, that I seemed to be lost and swallowed up in God. Blessed be the name of the Lord, I know that I am crucified to the world, and the world to me.

Sept. 10. Two friends, for whose conversion I have been most deeply interested, called today. They have both tasted that the Lord is good, and are now, with most grateful hearts, rejoicing in the God of their salvation. Since Mrs. ____'s conversion, which was but a week or two since, God has also given her

her husband to accompany her. He was a violent opposer, and when she asked permission to attend a special means of grace, two or three weeks since, with the secret hope of finding the Lord, his consent was very reluctantly given, fearing, as he said, that she would get a religion that would make her melancholy all her days. After some persuasion, he concluded to let her go. The Lord healed her wounded spirit while there, and she returned home very happy in the enjoyment of religion. On telling her husband of the gracious change, he became greatly enraged, and one; in the days of our Savior, under demoniacal influence, could scarcely have shown more malignity and deep-rooted hatred to the cause of Christ, than did this individual toward the cause that the beloved of his bosom had espoused. She had anticipated opposition; but little imagined the mighty storm which was to meet her, on thus disclosing the secret of her joy to him whom she ever had reason to regard as the friend of her happiness, her devoted husband. She knew not where the storm would end; but continued casting herself upon her almighty Savior for sustainment and succor in this her day of trouble. It was on Friday she told him of the happy change, and persecution raged with unabated fury until Saturday night, when, in his desperation, he loaded a pistol, and said that he would put an end to his existence, which had been rendered so miserable by the blighting of all his future prospects. But He who holdeth the tempest in his hand prevented the execution of his design.

Finding that his threats were powerless in moving her, he now began another course. "Do you believe in the Trinity?" he authoritatively demanded.

Yes," she meekly replied, "I do."

"And what reason have you for such a belief?" said he.

"The Bible teaches it," she responded, "and I believe all that is taught in the Bible."

He then denied his belief in the doctrine of the Trinity, but soon afterward became silent and began to weep, and continued to weep during the remainder of the night. Undetermined in her own mind as to the character of his sorrow, whether induced from excessive vexation, remorse, or penitence, she said nothing.

In the morning he informed her that he had not had one moment's peace since he denied his belief in the Trinity. "And now," said he, "since you will not go with me, I have made up my mind to go with you." He became an earnest seeker of salvation, and went with her that morning to the house of God.

In the afternoon they were detained, from some indisposition in the family, from attending church. He expressed to his beloved companion his resolute determination to lead a new life, and gave evidence of his sincerity by his expressions of godly sorrow, and bringing forth fruits meet for repentance. But she greatly feared his again mingling in business with his skeptical associates, to whom he would be exposed, and left him to pour out her soul in secret before God. On her leaving him, he took up the Bible, and opened on these words, "But thou, when thou prayest, enter into thy closet, and when thou hast shut thy door, pray to thy Father, which is in secret; and thy Father, which seeth in secret, shall reward thee openly." He felt that the Bible was the word of the Lord, and *really believed* the declaration that had been presented to him, and began to pray earnestly, and believingly, for the blessing implied; and God gave it, and made him a joyful witness of his pardoning mercy. When Mrs.____ returned to the room, he threw his arms around her neck, and declared what God had done for his soul. Thus was the lion, in a few short hours, transformed to the lamb.

"Is there a thing too hard for thee,
　　Almighty Lord of all;
Whose threatening looks dry up the sea,
　　And bid the mountains fall?"
Thursday, 13th. The Lord God omnipotent reigneth. Yes,

"Jesus reigns, he reigns victorious,
Over heaven and earth most glorious,
　　　　　　Jesus reigns."

He reigns triumphant in my soul. I at present enjoy, through his all-abounding grace, conscious victory over sin, death, and the grave. O, what a conquest over timid nature hath grace gained! Some time since, I said to my companion, when on the eve of retiring for the night, "The skeptic could scarcely conceive that the believer in Christ could feel such a perfect repose and confidence in him, that, on retiring to rest, he could say, I feel that I repose so confidently in the arms of Infinite Love, that it is matter of no solicitude whether I awake in time or in eternity — but I do indeed feel that I can say so." This day the observation has been brought forcibly to my remembrance by a singular dream I had last night. I thought three or four members of our family, with myself, were sitting together, when some one knocked for admittance. I invited the person in, when, to our surprise, a beloved brother, deceased about two years since, entered. Though we all seemed perfectly aware of the fact, that he was a visitant from the spiritual world, yet he seemed so pleased to see us, and greeted us in the same lovely, affectionate manner, so peculiar to him when in life, that we could not find it in our hearts to yield to anything like a repulsiveness of manner toward him, on account of the strangeness of the visitation. After presenting his hand, and giving an affectionate kiss to each, he came to me, and with still stronger marks of endearment than with the others, throwing his arms around my neck, with an indescribable look of fondness and affection, he said, "You will be with me...Sabbath," and immediately left the room. Consternation now sat on every countenance, and an awful silence ensued, which I was the first to break, by asking, "Did he say *on* Sabbath, or *after* Sabbath?" He had been so hasty in the delivery of his message that I had lost the word, and their consternation on hearing the announcement had been such that they had also failed to hear the *precise* time. From that time to the moment if my waking, which was seemingly — two or three hours, I was engaged in making preparations similar to those which would have been made had the dream been an actual announcement from the spiritual world. When I awoke it still lingered with the vividness of reality upon my mind. My feelings forbade my entering with zest into contemplations of the future, which the scenes around me were calculated to cherish. It was my impression that I was about to finish my earthly pilgrimage; and if so soon, it seemed but reasonable that my time should be spent in a manner to correspond with the momentousness of the circumstance. And yet it was a dream, and the idea of having my mind thus influenced by a mere dream I was fearful might appear visionary, and, give unnecessary uneasiness. Influenced by these considerations, I said but little; yet the circumstances in which my mind was placed, gave abundant opportunity to test the truth of the observations with which I commenced to write. Over and again it came to my mind during the morning, that the Lord might have permitted the trial to test the strength of the principle so confidently asserted on the evening alluded to; and blessed be the name of the Lord, it still continued *firm,* when brought to this trying test. About noon, something having a bearing on the future, needed a promptness of action, quite at variance with my impressions of speedy dissolution; and in endeavoring to draw nigh to God, in reference to the subject, I was permitted near and sweet access to the throne, while asking, that if this trial was intended as a sure intimation that I was done with the things of earth, the impression that it was indeed so might be deepened; but if it were only designed to test the confident belief expressed to my companion on the occasion referred to, it might be so removed that. I might feel that I had yet something to do with the world. A direct answer was given, and immediately I was assured that it had only been permitted to assume all the plausibility spoken of, in order to bring the most tangible evidence to my mind, that I had not been mistaken in the belief I had so confidently expressed.

October 13. I have just returned from a visit to B___. The Lord has been with me during my absence from my beloved family, and imparted the strong and increasingly-confirming consolations of his Spirit. I started on the 24th, and went through a journey of about two hundred miles in one day, with comfort. A sweet, heavenly calmness, pervaded my mind during the day. Aware that the multiplicity of scenes through which I should pass were calculated to dissipate the mind, I sought unto God, and was enabled to repose most confidently on my almighty Savior. I carried in my hand a little book, entitled the "Believers' Inheritance," being a compilation of precious promises. "An inheritance indeed," responded my soul, as I feasted upon the exceeding great and precious promises. I had prayed much that the glare of outward circumstance might not be permitted to break in upon the quiet of my soul. The petition was answered to a degree beyond my expectations.

Seldom in the quietness of my own room has the peace of God that passeth all understanding been more absorbingly realized. It seemed but to close my eyes on outward things, in order to be in no ordinary degree alone with God. It was to this heavenly serenity of soul that I attributed, mainly, the little fatigue of body I felt in accomplishing the journey.

I was enabled to urge the subject of religion earnestly on the ladies' maid of the cars. She became deeply interested, and I am in expectation of seeing fruit of my labor in the eternal world, to the praise of God. I have often been greatly encouraged in similar attempts to be instant in season and out of season. Eternity alone can disclose the amount of good that may be accomplished by Christ's "little ones," if only faithful in the improvement of small opportunities for doing good. What a noble example was the sainted Carvosso!

Sabbath, 25th. It rained during the morning, which prevented my going to the Lord's house. I found an effort necessary to ward off the propensity to ordinary, or every-day topics in those around me. I am thankful that the Lord has laid his hand on me in reference to this subject. From a child I was taught to sanctify the Sabbath, and my associations of good, whether in relation to temporal or spiritual prosperity, were most religiously blended with a careful observance of this hallowed day. The Lord so blessed early parental admonitions, and the instructions of his blessed word to my infant heart, that I can scarcely remember the time when I was not influenced by the opinion, that if I thought or conversed on topics of mere worldly interest, I need not expect prosperity in the prosecution of the matter in contemplation.

The Holy Spirit is just now urging upon my mind a period when this principle of right was so blended with that which was questionable, that it was hardly to be decided which way the scale at the time preponderated. I had been making quite extensive preparations for a New Year's festival. It was Saturday evening, December 31st. Fearful that I should be tempted to think my own thoughts on the Sabbath, if not all in readiness for the early calls anticipated on Monday, I concluded to forego the practice, to which I had been from childhood accustomed, of going to the sanctuary, and there, with the solemn assembly, renewing my covenant with God. But I thought I would most carefully devote the last hour of the expiring year to this purpose, at home. Before I was aware, I was admonished that but fifteen minutes remained, ere the new year would be ushered in; and the religious observances, which by the force of habit, I think, graciously formed, had become sacredly binding, still remained untouched. The Spirit, which had before been silently reproving, now chidingly appealed to my heart — "What! but this little remnant of the year to devote to the formation of new purposes, and the renewal of your covenant engagements with God?" It was my heavenly Father who reproved, and I felt most painfully oppressed and grieved, from a review of the manner in which his superior claim upon this important hour had been resisted, and I scarcely dared to look up for help in this my time of need. But the hand of God was upon me, and I felt that it would be but a greater triumph for the adversary should I desist from entering into those engagements. Scarcely had this point been settled, before another formidable barrier presented. It was the fearful possibility of breaking the engagements, by the temptations that might be anticipated from the diversified society in which I was expecting to mingle on Monday! "Better is it that thou shouldst not vow, than that thou shouldst vow and not pay," said the enemy! But the Spirit urged upon my mind the solemn duty of vowing to God, and a careful performance of my vows; and with this powerful conviction, took the blessed, word and knelt before the Lord, with an indescribable sense of responsibility weighing down my spirit, which was penetrated with an unusual consciousness of innate helplessness. I began to pour out my soul thus: "O Lord! if thou wilt but give me something from thy word, to strengthen and encourage me, I will, through thy grace assisting me, take whatever thou wilt give, as my motto during the coming year." I then opened on these words, "I can do all things through Christ, which strengtheneth me!" O how my soul bounded! The word of the Lord was indeed the power of God unto my soul; and scarcely could I have had a stronger realization that this was indeed the voice of God to me, had it been spoken from heaven to the outward ear, as well as to the inmost soul. I now with delightful elasticity and firmness of spirit renewed my covenant engagements, and formed new purposes; a prominent one of which was, that I would be more zealous for the Lord of hosts than I had ever before been; and would take the earliest opportunity to inform my friends of the decision, in order that the temptations to retreat might be cut off as speedily as possible. This was an important period in my pilgrimage, from which I never retraced my way back to that degree of worldly-mindedness that would invest the etiquette of the day with a vitality sufficiently inspiring or captivating to draw off the energies of the Christian to its pigmy pursuits. In reference to all such things, I *now* think that the royal heir of heaven stands in such a commanding attitude before the world, that the dignity of his station fully justifies him in saying, "I am engaged in a great work, and cannot come down."

In the afternoon, went to C___ street church. Heard Mr. D___ preach a truly evangelical sermon. Yet there was an apathy, and a feeling of irresponsibility manifested by the congregation, that were really painful to me to witness. During singing, I observed that about half the assembly were sitting, and the others standing. I have not taken special pains to inform myself of the most Scriptural method for the regulation of public worship, from the impression that these are not the "weightier matters of the law," but I do feel persuaded that there is not only moral unseemliness, but Scriptural impropriety, in the listlessness of demeanor indulged in by various denominations of the present day. I have gone into churches that differ in these non-essentials, with an intention of conforming to the usage peculiar to the order, and on doing so have found myself singled out from the majority of the worshipers, and have afterward concluded, that if my example could not be conducive to uniformity, I would act in the case in accordance with my views of Scriptural propriety; and though perhaps the only one in the whole assembly besides the minister, who, like God's ancient servant, was kneeling, and with outstretched hands supplicating the mercy-seat, I have turned and knelt, determined that I would not approach the Majesty of heaven in such an attitude as I would not dare approach an earthly sovereign. In respect to many particular points of duty, the Scriptures do not furnish explicit precepts, but they do most expressly regulate everything by some one great commanding truth; and thus in reference to this subject it has been said, "Let all things be done decently *and in order.*" And why should not this injunction be regarded as binding on individual professors? The same want of uniformity I have observed in other particulars among many who I think really love and revere the Sovereign of heaven and earth. Some will break in upon his worship, and attract the eye and heart of the unwary, by an unnecessarily late attendance. Others most unceremoniously place themselves in an attitude most favorable for repose, which would be regarded in ill taste in polite society. And should such unseemliness of action be indulged in in the presence of an earthly potentate, surely the aggressor would be spurned from his presence. And yet the avowed object of an attendance on the means of grace is to meet GOD — to worship and hold converse with him who is the blessed and only Potentate, the "King of kings and Lord of lords." Well might preachers of the present day say, with the preacher of olden time, "Keep thy foot when thou goest to the house of God," &c.

While at the meeting this afternoon, the Lord poured out the spirit of supplication upon me in an unusual manner. The cry of my heart was for a revival of Scriptural holiness in this place. It was a mighty struggle, but I was enabled, through the omnipotence of grace, to come off more than conqueror. I received the assurance that my petition had gone up before the throne, presented in the name of Jesus, and that I should have the desire of my heart.

Oct. 28. I went to meeting this evening with a soul longing for the courts of the Lord. There were but six or eight brethren present, and no females, with the exception of sisters E___ and myself. That faith that approaches near to God and claims *present* blessings seemed at a very low ebb. I do not think that one prayer or expression in anticipation of a present bestowment of the gift of holiness was uttered.

The expectations that were given in answer to the prayer of faith, on Sabbath afternoon, came forcibly to remembrance, and the inquiry was presented, "Are you willing to make every possible effort toward the accomplishment of this work?"

My soul replied, "I am not at my own disposal: body, soul and spirit, time talents, and influence, are thine:

"I'll follow on if thou command,
        All is well.'"

After joining in prayer, I told them of the manner in which my soul had been drawn out on Sabbath afternoon for a revival of holiness, and the way in which I felt the work might be accomplished, if they would but begin at once to be workers together with God, by having a commencement of it in the hearts of all present. I then stated, in a manner as concise as possible, the way in which the Lord had made me a witness of this grace — how it had affected me in reference to my usefulness to others, by the far more comprehensive views of responsibility which it had given me, and concluded by saying, that I could not but regard a revival in the hearts of God's professed people to be the necessary foundation for a thorough revival of the work of God in all its departments.

After I had finished, a brother arose and confessed that, some years since, he had been the happy possessor of the blessing of holiness, but did not long retain it, and knew, from experience, that it was, as the sister had said, just what was needed for our own happiness and safety, and also to capacitate us for usefulness to others, — and necessary in the church, as the foundation for a revival — and that he now felt unwilling to live any longer without it. He then earnestly asked all present to pray for him, that he might again be brought into the enjoyment of the blessing. The spirit of the meeting was greatly revived.

Oct. 30. Called today on a Christian brother, who has been exercised with severe affliction for several years past. We had a season of sweet refreshing, while conversing of the things that appertain to the kingdom; and also in prayer and supplication, with thanksgiving, God was eminently near. Two young ladies, professors, who were present, acknowledged that they were following God at a distance, and were greatly aroused, and resolved on endeavoring to live nearer to God.

While at supper, after our return, I was appealed to for a decision on a peculiar case. The name of a person of undoubted piety was mentioned, who had a short time previous lost a son at a distance from home. He had been a source of much painful solicitude, on account of his profligate habits, and was overtaken by death, at an unlooked-for hour, and left no evidence of having been truly regenerated. The fond mother, agonized at the thought of his having died unprepared, cried constantly to the Lord for some assurance of his safety, and on one occasion, while thus pleading, she became confident in her own mind that prayer was answered, and the perfect assurance given of his happiness. Two or three unconverted persons being present, I felt a sacred responsibility in giving an opinion, and was constrained to dissent from the sister, from the fact that she had started from wrong premises at the outset. Had she remembered that "secret things belong to God, and those that are revealed to ourselves and children," she would have seen that it was her province to be satisfied with the allotments of divine Providence, assured that the Judge of all the earth will do right. There are unalterable principles laid down in the word of God, by which the character of our requests must be regulated, or they are not recognized in the court of heaven. "This is the confidence we have in him, that if we ask anything *according to his will,* he *heareth us.*" This *will* is given in the *written* word. Any prayer that is not according to this, I can conceive of no shade of Scriptural propriety in presenting before the Lord. Such an applicant cannot have his plea so much as entered before the throne. The sword of the Spirit prevents access to the Judge, by the sentence, "to the law and to the testimony."

I know it may be said, that persons of undoubted piety (as of the sister in question) have had remarkable answers to prayer similar to that just given, and some, of whom I have heard, have received answers in what they have conceived to be a miraculous manner, in dreams, &c., that have been equally at *variance* with the Spirit of the word. At once they wrap themselves in the security of the belief thus attained, from the assurance that it was given in *answer to prayer.* Such persons are unmindful of the fact, that if they wander in any degree from the direct way, marked out in the only chart God has given, they are left exposed to any infatuation that an insatiable, exceedingly subtle enemy can invent. The higher the profession and weight of religious influence, the more extensive and commanding the harm. Is it impossible that an enemy, who even quoted Scripture to the Savior, to suit his purpose, can so transform himself into an angel of light, as to answer a prayer which had its origin on his own premises? and if it is off the direct line of the written word, it surely is in a proportionate degree on his own ground, and however startling the truth, it is but *reasonable* to expect that he would respond, and answer it in just the way that would be likely to assume the most plausibility. I have really thought that Satan made use of a stratagem to keep some persons from continuing to agonize for their unconverted friends, by instigating them to pray for the assurance that they would eventually be saved. The answer is given — and the agony ceases. Meanwhile the friends continue sinning, and the WORD continues to declare, "The soul that sinneth, it shall die." The error lies in over-leaping the bounds God hath set. And when this is done, delusion is inevitable. There is no subject relative to which I have more ardently desired to be a *living epistle,* than in reference to the infinite importance, excellency, and comprehensiveness of the word of God. I do indeed regard it as a sufficient rule for faith and practice. I wonder why the absolute importance of searching the Scriptures, in order, by a careful study, to show ourselves approved in the sight of God and man, is not more urged, from the pulpit and the press.

We have no right to think that we shall be "thoroughly furnished unto every good work," or to conceive ourselves otherwise than liable to be carried about by every wind of doctrine, without a careful *searching* and "comparing of scripture with scripture," which surely implies something more than mere reading. And I most conscientiously believe, and my feelings and judgment bear me out in affirming, that there is no subject relative to which the world of professing Christians, on waking up in the spiritual world, will find themselves to have been more mistaken than in reference to this. It seems to me as if the various subterfuges to which men of otherwise enlightened judgment betake themselves as a substitute for the blessed word, must indeed be most amazing in the eyes of those spiritual intelligences by which we are surrounded. What a strange, God-dishonoring position it is, to acknowledge the Bible as the word of God, and yet suffer ourselves to be governed by our own feelings — the views, experience, and traditions of others, in reference to it, while we are every moment liable to be called into the other world, to answer for ourselves, and be judged by our individual conformity to its precepts! But are we to reject all manifestations from God, or answers to prayer, that may be given in dreams or visions of the night? The spirit of the word settles this matter. From the earliest, down to the latest period, God hath spoken to his people in this manner. As well might we deny any other part of divine revelation, as to deny this. Witness:— God said to Abraham in a dream, "Yea, I know thou didst this in the integrity of thy heart," &c. Genesis xx, 6. Jacob had a dream in Bethel of the ladder that reached from earth to heaven. "And the Lord stood above it, and said, I am the Lord God of Abraham thy father," &c. Gen. xxviii, 10-15. Jacob tells Laban of yet another time when God spoke to him in a dream on a subject quite dissimilar from the former. Gen. xxxi, 11-13. And to show that God does not confine his communications to his chosen people, he speaks to Laban in a dream, and says to him, "Take heed that thou speak not to Jacob, either good or bad." Ver. 24. God spake to the butler and baker. Gen. xl. Also to Pharaoh. Gen. xli. God speaking to Aaron and Miriam, says, "If there be a prophet among you, I the Lord will make myself known unto him in a vision, and will speak unto him in a dream," &c. "The Lord appeared unto Solomon in a dream by night, and said, Ask what I shall give thee." Solomon made his choice, and God granted his request, and "he awoke, and behold it was a dream!" 1 Kings iii, 5-15. Nebuchadnezzar (Daniel iv) and the wife of Pilate (Matt. xxvii, 1 9) were forewarned by God of impending judgments by a dream. "An angel appeared to Joseph in a dream, saying, Joseph, thou son of David, fear not," &c. Matt. i, 20. The wise men were "warned of God in a dream, that they should not return to Herod." Matt. ii, 12. "An angel of the Lord appeared in a dream to Joseph, in Egypt." Matt. ii, 19. But why enumerate? Most explicit declarations from God place the matter beyond doubt. "For God speaketh once, yea twice, yet man perceiveth it not. In a dream, in a vision of the night, when deep sleep falleth upon men, in slumberings upon the bed: then he openeth the ears of men, and sealeth their instruction, that he may withdraw man from his purpose, and hide pride from man." Job xxxiii, 14-17.

Early under the Christian dispensation, God invested the subject with still higher claims, if possible, upon the attention of man, by the declaration, "And it shall come to pass in the last days, saith God, I will pour out my Spirit upon all flesh; and your sons and your daughters shall prophesy, and your young men shall see visions, and your old men shall dream dreams."

And yet the subject, though standing in such a commanding attitude, is seemingly liable to so much abuse, that it has become disreputable for God's servants to say, in the present day, "God spake to me in a dream, or vision of the night." And why is it thus? Is it not because the SCRIPTURE (the plain, naked word of God) is not brought to the ordeal of a personal, diligent, careful investigation? Books of every diversity of sentiment, and men of every manner of opinion are consulted, and then the precious, neglected, insulted WORD, is too often submitted to the ordeal thus erroneously begotten. I here most solemnly protest, "in the sight of God who quickeneth all things, and before Jesus Christ," that in obedience to the most confirmed convictions of duty, from the awful deference and honor due the HOLY SPIRIT, I have felt sacredly bound, in preparing myself for my Bible class exercises, and in the devotions of the closet, first to take the naked, unadorned word upon my knees in the presence of God, in order to have my mind primarily preoccupied with the teachings of the Holy Spirit, *before* it was submitted to the dictations of men, however learned or good. With deep abasement before God, I would also state, that not infrequently I have gone as a simple little child, conscious of perfect ignorance, and of a liability to embrace the most egregious error, if left one moment unprotected by a superior wisdom and guidance; and believing that "all Scripture is given by inspiration, and is profitable for *doctrine,* reproof, correction, and instruction in righteousness," have asked, relative to portions of the word that I could not at once apprehend, direct and special illumination, and it has been given. After having thus sought unto God, I have conscientiously made use of every available help, and God has blessed me greatly in meeting with sentiments not only corroborative of those already received, but also helpful toward still further illumination.

Some who may have been despoiled of some long-cherished hope, by the promulgation of such sentiments as those with which I commenced my present reflections, may be disposed to say, perchance chidingly, as anticipated in ancient time, (Deut. xviii, 21,) "How shall we know the word which the Lord hath not spoken," if expectations so *sincerely* begotten, are so exceedingly dubious? The ever-unalterable principles regulating the government of God, as laid down in the WORD, are so distinct, compact, and comprehensive, that I have never yet, in all my experience, found one case but what has been touched, neither do I ever expect to find one; and were I expecting my pilgrimage to be lengthened out to the age of Methuselah, and temptations from the world, the flesh, and Satan, to increase continually in poignancy, and subtlety of invention, and spirits of darkness to thicken in numbers, for the mighty conflict, I think I should not need any other shield or weapon than the word of God — the sword of the Spirit. Furnished with this, every man is invested with power, not only to fight his own battles, but to plead his own cause. How unlike earthly tribunals is the court of heaven? It is seldom we hear of an individual sufficiently acquainted with the technicalities of law to assume the responsibility of pleading his own cause, and few are possessed of the faculties, had they the disposition; but here, with the Holy Spirit for his teacher, the most humble believer may, by having skillfully wielded the sword of the Spirit, and made his way through every conceivable difficulty, come up thus thoroughly furnished before the throne — present his cause, and be as truly shielded from insult, neglect, or rejection, as though he were clothed with the person of Christ. Scriptural demonstration asserts that he is clothed with Christ. Shielded by the atonement, he is in verity as impervious to the assaults of the enemy, as He who is called in the ever-blessed Bible; "THE FAITHFUL AND TRUE WITNESS — THE WORD OF GOD."

Tuesday. I again attended Rev. Mr.____'s class. The Lord has doubtless commenced a good work in very many souls here, but it is surprising that I hear so little about holiness, as a present attainment, or as within the reach of the believer,, as though it were not a distinctive feature in our economy. The fact of its being so, is surely a tremendous consideration. It was asked in ancient time, "What profit hath the Jew?" and the reply, "*Much every way,*" is surely an answer that should sink with fearful weight into the ear and heart of every Methodist, circumstanced as we are in the order of God, in reference to this subject. The fact of having received, from God, through such men as Wesley, Fletcher, Nelson, Bramwell, and a host of other heaven-owned luminaries, this glorious doctrine, as revealed in the blessed word, throws a weight of responsibility, most tremendous in magnitude, upon our ministry and people.

I sometimes fear that the nature and depth of the obligations thus imposed will not be fully realized until the clear light of eternity shall disclose the subject in all its bearings. I verily believe that when God thrust the Wesleys out to raise a holy people, and we became a distinct organization, with men of such simple, childlike, enlightened and yet noble piety, under God, at the head of our ecclesiastical affairs, that he really intended that we should retain more of those distinctive features by which our economy is characterized, as dissimilar in doctrine and usage from other evangelical bodies. I know it is thought by many of our warm admirers, that we, as a people, have but received the polish inevitable from oft-repeated usage, having only lost in that which was deemed unseemly and rough, and quite unsuited to the enterprise of the age. If the refining fire — the Spirit of holiness — were more signally blended with all our operations, and lighting down upon our assemblies more now, than in ancient time, I might think so too; but it is the Spirit that giveth life, and that Spirit can only be cherished by the unostentatious, careful, humble, childlike dependence on God, that led the fathers of Methodism to discountenance the glare of the world — that made Wesley say, by precept and example, that he was afraid of the rich, not but that he would tolerate them, for some of his friends were the titled dignitaries of the day; but the tide of mere worldly popularity, it is well known, he took the utmost pains to ward off. Weight in piety, not in numbers, was the design most evident, and the most striking feature standing out on the face of the economy of which he was, under God, the originator.

Rev. Mr.___, the pastor of this charge, has been on my mind almost day and night, since the first of my coming to this place. He is an able minister of the New Testament, but O! how much he needs that his lips should be touched with a live coal from off the hallowed altar! The more I trace the hand of God in his usual mode of working with the people, the more I see the necessity of his appointed ambassadors being experimental witnesses of the attainableness of what they proclaim. The experience of one such goes further toward bringing others on the same ground, than the most labored theories of many, unable to say, "We speak that we know, and testify of that we have seen."

A pleasing exhibition of the justness of these observations was given me by a beloved friend. in the statement of her experience. Her early religious associations were with a denomination unfavorable to the doctrine of holiness as admitted by our people. But she began to seek most earnestly for a state of entire conformity to the will of God, and having been informed that there was a people who held to the possibility of attaining such a state, she sought them out, and united in church fellowship with them. She now heard holiness spoken of as a Bible doctrine, and her soul was greatly strengthened and encouraged in the pursuit, yet she earnestly desired to hear some one say, *"I know it — I feel it."*

At length her wish was gratified. She had resorted to a camp meeting with the hope of being more fully informed, not only by pulpit ministration, and Biblical exposition, but by the concurrence of *living* testimony; and it was for the latter that she most greatly longed. Her heart had already assented to the commanding truth that holiness is a Bible doctrine. The Lord in great mercy moved the spirit of one of his chosen servants to discourse most sweetly on the nature and privilege of a state of holiness. "O," thought she, "if I could only now hear him say, 'I *enjoy it*,' I should be satisfied."

Soon afterward, as if moved by a divine impulse, with a holy heroism he lifted up to the gaze of the eager multitude the chart containing his commission — the Book of books. "O," said he, "I do not only proclaim this glorious doctrine to you from *this* blessed book, but I have it *here,*" -and then reaching forth the Bible toward the weeping assembly, and placing his hand upon a heart bursting with emotion, he repeated — "*I have it here.*" "It is enough," she exclaimed. That evening, her longing soul was brought into the way of holiness.

One evening this week, I met with Mrs. ___, a person of sincere piety, with whom I think I should have enjoyed unmingled pleasure, had it not been for her propensity to indulge in the habit of speaking lightly of the ministry. I revere the sacred office. I fully believe that our ministry generally have been moved by the Holy Ghost to preach the gospel. If so, they are invested with responsibilities of infinite magnitude. As ambassadors from the court of heaven, they receive their commission from the King of kings. An ambassador from an earthly monarch is deemed honorable according to the degree of responsibility with which he is invested, and the dignity of the throne which he represents, and to which he is amenable for a faithful delivery of his embassy. An ignominious reception of his message, or dishonor cast upon his person, is regarded as done unto the throne which he represents. and thus, doubtless, will the King of heaven hold those individuals or communities responsible who lightly esteem or disadvantageously speak of those legally-authorized ambassadors from the court of heaven, whom he hath commissioned to stand in Christ's stead, to beseech men to be reconciled to God.

The day of eternity will doubtless reveal that many a message of mercy has been rejected by the lost sinner, from the fact that his heart had been rendered impervious by slanderous reports or whisperings of "lowness of piety," or nameless disqualifications some of which may have gained currency, or received the sanction of silence from those who profess the name of Christ. God has assured my heart that men are answerable for truth, from whatever source it comes; and in reference to those whom he hath anointed and sent forth to preach the everlasting gospel, he hath written upon my inmost soul, "Touch not mine anointed, and do my prophets no harm." From an indulgence in this evil, many unquestionably suffer the displeasure of the King of glory, bring barrenness upon their own souls, and incur the awful responsibility of being instrumental of inducing a rejection of God's message.

On Tuesday evening, Miss ___, an amiable young lady, called to see me. Her mind has been deeply interested for some time on the subject of holiness. I lifted my heart to the Lord for a word in season, and God gave an immediate answer. I was quite unacquainted with her circumstances in life, and consequently unapprised of the temptations peculiar to her case, but began to assure her of the faithfulness of God, in the speedy performance of his own part of the work, as soon as she was willing to comply with the conditions. I then related to her the experience of a young lady, with whom I had been familiar, who seemed greatly to desire the blessing of holiness; but on trying to pray with her for a present bestowment of the blessing, I could feel no liberty, and became assured in my own mind that some insuperable barrier was standing between God and her soul. With much hesitation, she afterward informed me that she was contemplating a marriage engagement with a young gentleman not professing religion. The mystery was at once solved, and I assured her that unless it was already made, her aspirations for present holiness and future felicity also would be futile, if she persisted in the prosecution of the affair. She received the statement of my views with a heavy heart, and I feared that this important crisis in her experience was to be but the turning point for a fearful plunge into the fatal vortex of mere worldly-minded profession. But grace ordered it otherwise; the struggle ended the next evening - the idol was given up, and the victory was, beyond expectation, glorious. The Lord condescended to take her into very close communion with himself, and she really looked as if the signature of God, the stamp of holiness, had been written upon her very countenance; and from that time, she became a decided, zealous, and useful traveler in the King's highway.

While I was giving this recital to the interesting young friend, her countenance bespoke a heart greatly disquieted, and, with much embarrassment, she informed me that a case of precisely the same interest was pending with herself. At once I saw that the Lord had indeed. in answer to prayer, given "a word in. season." The advice was made instrumental in frustrating the designs of the tempter, — her feet were turned from the vortex, which had been well-nigh reached, and she also became a happy, and useful, and deeply-interesting traveler in the King's highway.

Wednesday. The election of city officers has been so intensely absorbing with every class of the community, since I have been here, that but little time has been left for conversation on any other subject. I have been thinking if we could take the interest manifested by the Christian community apart, and concentrate it on some definite pursuit of praiseworthy benevolence — say, to the promotion of a revival, in personal or individual experience — what glorious results might follow! Doubtless it would terminate in many a name being enrolled under the banner of Immanuel — in the book of life — and in many an election being made sure which before was exceedingly dubious.

I do not object to Christians zealously interesting themselves on the subject of appointing "the powers that be." If the Scriptures enjoin the duty of not resisting them, surely it is greatly desirable to have such as our Christian judgment can acknowledge to be "ministers of God to us for good." But how few professors seem to apprehend the obligation imposed by apostolic exhortation, "that first of all, supplications, prayers, intercessions, and giving of thanks, be made for all men for all that are in authority, that we may lend a quiet and peaceable life!" They seem to forget that the powers that be are ordained by God, and also of the divine injunction, "Speak evil of no man," and act upon the assumption that they are to make use of the same carnal weapons, and wield them also in the same manner as is practiced by the mere worldling. May it not be in part attributable to these mistaken views and conduct, that few Christian men go through the ordeal of zealous electioneering, or an election to office, unharmed by the fire?

Sabbath. This was a day of extraordinary trial. My ever-watchful foe seemed to have found out new premises to work upon. I really felt as if continually surrounded by

"Legions of dire, malicious fiends."

The main effort on the part of my enemies was directed toward the answer to prayer which I had received for a revival of the work of holiness in this place on the first Sabbath after I came here. I had not yet seen, as evidently as had anticipated, the answer to my prayer, and this was the ground that the enemy took to work upon. Never before do I remember to have felt the necessity of looking well to the things I had prospectively gained by way of answer to prayer, in reference to others, as well as to blessings in actual possession. The contest continued with unabated fury until late at night, and my enemies would have intimidated me from taking the repose which my health much needed, by the insinuation that I should yet be despoiled of my confidence, had it not been for the inspiring hope given by the blessed word, assuring me that more were they that were for me, than all that were against me. The Captain of my salvation — the Lord of hosts — my condescending God — gave me a signal and glorious victory during my sleep.

I dreamed that I was at a church which I had not been accustomed to attend in this place the seats were densely crowded with an assembly of fervent worshipers, all silently, yet with unutterable intensity, supplicating God. The hour had arrived when I must depart, and I arose amid the praying multitude, as one alone to leave. Instead of going out in the usual way, passed up the aisle to the altar, where, to my astonishment, several kneeling suppliants were bowed, earnestly groaning in subdued tones for the blessing of holiness. I was much moved at the unexpected sight, and exclaimed, "What! all this and I not know it?" I rejoiced in spirit, and endeavored to encourage them, so long as my haste would permit, and then passed along before the altar, with the intention of going down the extreme aisle to the door, when my progress was again impeded by a still larger and yet more fervent company of suppliants, all imploring in unutterable groanings the blessing of holiness. I was almost overcome with wonder and gratitude, and exclaimed, "Can it be?" when the Spirit said to my heart, "This is the answer to your prayer!" It was too much, and I sat down and gave vent to my overwhelming joy in tears — when one most beseechingly said, "O sister ___," calling me by name, "do pray," and the vision fled. Joy unspeakable and full of glory now filled my soul. Every enemy was vanquished, and not one lingering temptation left to doubt that God had heard and was already answering my prayer.

On Monday evening I attended love-feast in ___ street church. The individual for whom I had been so prayerfully interested during the whole of my visit, and very especially during the evening, rose at the close of the meeting to speak. Had he been invested with power to read the emotions of my heart for the several preceding days, and during the evening, and then sought words to express those emotions, he could scarcely have said anything more satisfactory, with the exception that he had not yet received the witness (Note: soon afterward, he received the direct assurance, and was instrumental in an extensive revival of the work of God.) of holiness. The Lord had given me the earnest during the night previous, but now the full tide of joy ran so high, that my soul was unutterably filled with glory and with God. Soon afterward, he received the direct assurance, and was instrumental in an extensive revival of the work of God.

That night, on my return home, I was taken unexpectedly ill. The symptoms were so alarming that I began to anticipate the trial of being unable to reach my beloved home. I realized a perfect resignation to the will of God, but felt that he did not chide me when I asked, that if consistent with his will, the hand of disease might be arrested, that I might be permitted to undertake my contemplated journey homeward on the morrow.

The Lord heard and answered the petition, and I found myself surprisingly better in the morning, and quite able to undertake the journey. Yet the state of my health since my return has been quite precarious, and I am brought to the test of being willing to *suffer* as well as to *do* the will of God. The circumstances of my health, and the peculiar trials by which my faith has been exercised of late, have inclined me to feel as if the Lord was about to take me home. To the glory of his grace, I can state that I have not one *wish* apart from the will of God. He is my all in all -the center of my existence — the Alpha and the Omega — the beginning and the end — the first and the last.

Nov. 11. I feel in blessed realization that I dwell in God. He that abideth in the doctrine of Christ, hath both the Father and the Son. The Spirit taketh of the things of God, and revealeth them unto me, and I enjoy a blessed consciousness that I am not only enabled to abide in the doctrine of Christ, but daily to become more established, and my heart is indeed made the abode of the Triune Deity.

Should the veil of mortality at any moment fall, and introduce me into the sensible presence of Him whom my soul loveth, it seems to me as if my enraptured spirit could not be taken by surprise; heaven appears to be so nearly allied to earth. And is it indeed so! Am I so *near* to Jesus, and angels, and glorified spirits?

O yes! the blessed word even now most assuringly whispers the certainty to my heart — the sure word of prophecy — the voice of revelation tells me, that these blessed assurances are not the mere imaginings of an over-excited mind. Blessed beyond all that the mind can conceive is the state of that soul, who, through the blood of the everlasting covenant, hath entered within the veil. "Ye *are* come unto Mount Zion, and unto the city of the living God, the heavenly Jerusalem, and to an innumerable company of angels, to the general assembly and church of the first-born, which are written in heaven, and to God the judge of all, and to the. spirits of just men made perfect, and to Jesus the mediator of the new covenant, and to the blood of sprinkling." Who can portray the glory of the believer's inheritance, even on this side Jordan! There is a rest for the people of God, and we who believe *do* enter into rest:

"A land of rest from inbred sin,
A land of perfect holiness."

O the impotence of words! how inadequately does mortal language avail toward describing the privileges — the rich immunities — the unending felicities, of the happy believer, who has had "boldness to enter into the holiest by the blood of Jesus, by a new and living way which he hath consecrated for us through the veil!" *Abiding* here, "thy sun shall no more go down; neither shall thy moon withdraw itself for the Lord shall be thy light." "No more shall thy land be termed Desolate; but thou shalt be called Hepzibah, and thy land

Beulah: for the Lord delighteth in thee, and thy land shall be married." Yes, *married — united in everlasting oneness with Christ.*

Ever since I entered into the way of holiness, I have been blessed with the *abiding* presence of my Savior. I do not mean that I have always had equally *sensible* assurances of his love; yet I have not seen one moment since, when I have not known that the Sun of righteousness was shining upon my heart; and I have been enabled to testify that my Savior was with me, working in me to will and do his good pleasure; and conscious that the trial of my faith was *precious,* I have even *rejoiced* in tribulation. Often have I thought of this delightsome land, as Pilgrim's land of Beulah. The sun does not go down by day, neither doth the moon withdraw her light. O for power to exhibit its blessedness, and by my life to bring forth its fruits!

Nov. 13. I have been encouraged in my endeavors to be instant in season and out of season, by the experience of brother W___ a member of my husband's class. He had been telling the manner in which he had directed a penitent to Christ, and exhibited much clearness of views in explaining faith to the humble seeker.

Brother W___ had for some time been an earnest inquirer after full salvation, and only needed to carry out in his experience the same views he had presented to the penitent. I felt that I could almost upbraid him with the suggestion, that he required more faith of the penitent than he was himself willing to exercise. He acknowledged his error.

While I was asking if he was now willing to present *all,* whether known or *unknown,* he detected just where his failure had been. He had found but little difficulty in offering up all to God, as far as he knew, but he imagined something in the future, or something unknown, which possibly might not have been given up. That evening, on returning from the class-room, he was enabled to present all, whether known or unknown, resolved to trust for the present, and leave the future with God. With that violence which the kingdom of heaven *suffereth,* he was enabled to lay hold upon the promise, "I will receive you," and at once felt that he was sanctified through the belief of the truth. "Sanctify them through thy truth," was now a prayer most understandingly apprehended in his experience. On laying hold upon this promise, he found the word of the immutable Jehovah possessed of a soul-quickening, sin-destroying power. In *keeping* hold of it, he proved that there was virtue in the very touch, and its renovating influence ran through soul and body. In continuing to grasp it with a holy violence, the truth, as to the manner by which he, as a worker together with God, was to cleanse *himself* from all filthiness of the flesh and spirit, and perfect holiness in the fear of God, was sweetly opened to his understanding. He could now sing in a manner not before apprehended,

> "I cannot wash my heart,
> But by believing thee."

On Thursday evening last he bore a noble testimony in class-meeting, and bids fair to be very helpful in leading others into the way of holiness. How strange that such indefinite views, relative to the *duty* of believing, should prevail! If God had left it *optional* with ourselves, whether we would believe or otherwise, then there were some excuse for this indefiniteness and long lingering.

But now that God. hath placed the promises fully within our reach, and saith the WORD is nigh thee, "even *in* thy mouth, and *in thy heart*," and in most explicit admonition instructs as to the manner in which we are to use this precious word and prove its efficiency — "*Having* these promises, dearly beloved, let us *cleanse ourselves* from all filthiness of the flesh and spirit, perfecting holiness in the fear of God" — what excuse remains for so much indefiniteness relative to the enjoyment of holiness! I know it is a common observation, that "this and the other individual *must enjoy* a state of holiness, though from an unconsciousness of it they do not profess it." But how can these individuals cleanse themselves from all filthiness of the flesh and spirit, unless they lay hold upon the promises? and to lay hold upon them implies an act on the part of the creature, which he *cannot* be unconscious of. That violence must be used which the kingdom of heaven suffereth, —

"The heavenly kingdom suffers *force* -
'Tis seized with violent hands."

And can this force be exercised without a consciousness on the part of the individual, when

"Legions of wily fiends oppose?"

Can he *lay hold,* and *maintain* the shield of faith with an indefiniteness of feeling, and expression, which the fact of never saying anything about it would seem to imply?

I must confess, when it is said to me, "Such a person *must* enjoy the blessing, though he may not *know* it; or, he must enjoy the blessing, although he does not profess it," &c., I cannot well understand: I must be better informed relative to the Bible mode of *attaining* and *retaining,* before I can believe it.

For a long time past it has been a solemn, settled conviction with me, that the reason why more sincerely pious persons do not attain the witness that the blood of Jesus cleanseth, is for want of bringing the matter to a point, and then deciding with energy and perseverance, I *must* and *will* have it *now*. Many, doubtless, standing in an official relation to Christ's visible body, where important trusts are committed, sincerely conceive that their diversified cares will not admit of absorption in these that may be deemed minor points in individual experience. Had the Wesleys or a Fletcher thought so, what a glorious doctrine might still have been withheld from the world! And now that a mighty people hath been raised through their instrumentality; a people whose distinctive peculiarity is their belief in the attainableness of *holiness* in the present life; can any matter, however extensive in bearing, stand in such close, vital connection with the well-being of the church as this? The more influential the station, the more commanding is the demand for explicit personal testimony. When Wesley, in his first conferences, made the subject of sanctification matter of earliest investigation and admonition, had a subtle reasoner said, "It is true, that you, as the founder of this sect, have ever presented the attainment of holiness in the present life as one of your fundamental principles, but you have never given us any reason to believe that you have *experimentally proved* its attainableness in the present life;" would not his admonitions have been comparatively futile?

The Savior gives a lesson on the importance of earnestness and explicitness: "Which of you shall have a friend, and shall go unto him at *midnight,* and say unto him, Friend, lend me *three* loaves." Notwithstanding the unseasonableness of the hour, and the unwillingness of your friend, you continue to importune, until at last your friend rises and gives *just* as many as you need. As much as if the Savior had said, *Ask* for precisely what you need, *importune* for it, and then expect the identical thing which you have asked for. "If a son shall ask *bread* of any of you that is a father, will be give him a *stone?*" But it is not implied that this petitioner would have received just what he desired had he been less importunate or less explicit.

How truly have I had occasion to observe that God is no respecter of persons in dispensing his gifts! I have seen those occupying an exalted position in the religious and literary world, manifesting the docility of a little child, willingly and even gladly submitting to the simple dictations of the most humble disciples of Jesus.

I knew one who had for many years made theology an absorbing study, and had wrapped himself in almost unapproachable dignity, who became convinced, mainly from reading the Scriptures, that holiness is a Bible doctrine. He knew of a denomination, whom in his heart he had despised, who held holiness as an important doctrine in their creed, and in humbleness of mind he hastened to a minister of that denomination, and asked to be directed to a witness of holiness. The minister manifested some embarrassment, and then said, 'To speak candidly, sir, I do not encourage my people in explicit testimony on this subject. *One* of my members makes the profession of living in the enjoyment of this state, but she is at present away on a visit from this place."

The disappointed theologian turned away grieved and astonished; but truth had taken hold upon his mind, and the disappointment, though vexatious, did not wholly paralyze his energies, or unsettle his belief in holiness as a Bible doctrine.

Some time afterward, several ministers of his own denomination, likeminded with himself, convened a meeting in order to obtain explicit testimony on the subject. One of the Savior's little ones, hearing of the convention, went, and gave in a simple, unsophisticated testimony, relative to the manner in which she had been brought to prove Christ as a Savior, able to save to the uttermost. The Lord made the simple testimony a word in season to the theologian. Weeks intervened, but the humble testimony continued absorbingly before his mind. He returned to the city, where the female resided, and sought out her abode.

She again presented the way of simple faith, and told him when he actually came to the point and laid all upon the altar, it was his duty to lay hold upon the promise, "I will receive you." he did lay hold, and spent almost the entire of that night, the next day, and the ensuing night, in laboring to assure his heart before God. It seemed as if principalities and powers were

"In mighty phalanx join'd,"

to withstand him, and to wrest from him the shield of faith. Ever and anon, during this severe trial of his faith, as he was tempted to unloose his grasp, the Spirit would appealingly say, *"He that believeth not, maketh God a liar!"* and fear of the awful sin of unbelief deterred him from yielding the point. On the third day, a perfect calm succeeded, and peace reigned throughout all his borders, every enemy was vanquished, and Christ was *all in all*.

On the same day he went to an assembly of divines, and with other lovers of holiness, who convened in a neighboring city, told them of the mighty victory of faith; and through his testimony on that day another theologian entered into the rest of perfect love.

Conversing with a minister on one occasion, who had long felt it his duty to *believe,* and enter into the rest of perfect love, he acknowledged that he saw *but one way* of entering into the enjoyment of the blessing. I had just been presenting that one way, and he replied, —

"I know that it is indeed just so: *there is no other way;* and I often think how it would be with me, if I knew I was about to pass into the other world. I know 'without holiness no man shall see the Lord,' and it seems to me as if I should then, with a desperate venture, throw myself upon the infinite merit of the atonement; and I *know I should be fully saved*. I often ask myself, why I cannot do it *now?* but I cannot bring myself to the point. Something seems to hinder, as though it were impossible; and yet I know it is not."

I said in return:— "Unless you make this desperate venture, brother, you will never be a witness of the power of Christ to save unto the uttermost. All who have been brought into a state of full salvation have had to make it; and unless you bring yourself to this desperate venture, which you anticipate in the hour of death, at an earlier period, the cause of holiness will be robbed of your testimony. Many, not half as willing to be holy as yourself, convinced of your sincerity as a seeker of full salvation, will conclude, from your example, that the command, 'Be ye holy,' is hard to be complied with, and will give the matter up in discouragement; and thus instead of saying, by your persuasive example, 'We are well able to go up and possess the good land,' you, as did the unbelieving spies, will also exercise a dissuasive influence."

Years have since passed, and that brother still occupies the same disheartening position.

November 14. Yesterday, temptations ran high, but, by the power of all-conquering grace, I was sustained. The suggestion was continually urged upon my mind that I had in some way unknowingly offended. I was enabled to keep hold on the word. "If in anything ye be otherwise minded, God will reveal even this unto you." My heart was continually saying, "Though I die, will I not remove my integrity from me." In my tribulation I was not left utterly joyless. Hope as an anchor continued steadfast within the veil. Though the buffetings from my enemy were continual and severe, yet he did not succeed once in fastening condemnation on my mind. I constantly and consciously kept all upon the altar, and,

"In hope believing against hope,"

succeeded, through the skill of my heavenly Pilot, in weathering out the storm. On this occasion, I was assailed with a variety of temptations, new and perplexing, but already have I proved the trial of my faith "precious." New lessons of grace have been learned, which I greatly prize. Thus it is that the wrath of my enemies praises Him. In how many ways does the Lord permit me to prove that his "word is TRUTH!"

December 13. "I think the Lord requires so much faith of me," said a dear sister, today. She had indeed been exercised with very severe trials. I took sweet satisfaction in assuring her that God never tries grace which he has not given. I endeavored to go through with an enumeration of the trials of Abraham's faith, for the admonition of this dear friend, and seldom have felt my own heart more instructed and strengthened than on this occasion, in reviewing the example of the father of the faithful. We were mutually encouraged by the example of him who, being dead, yet speaketh, and with higher hopes, and stronger faith, resolved to

"...travel all the length
Of the celestial road."

The case of this friend is in several respects very instructive. She is possessed of more than ordinary intelligence, but for several years was a confirmed infidel. She became skeptical from observing the little effect a profession of religion had on the mind and habits of professors. In her youthful days, she was for some time united in church fellowship with a denomination where a profession of holiness would have been thought fanatical. She took a deliberate survey of the religion of the Bible, its demands and promises, and felt that her own experience was not answerable to it, and on looking-on the mass of professors by which she was surrounded, she saw so little to authorize the idea that they really *believed* what they professed, that she gradually gave way to infidelity. About two years since, she fell in the way of my husband in one of his professional visits. Her case furnishes a striking confutation of the idea that the doctrine of holiness cannot be understood or appreciated by the unbeliever. He was in the sick room of a professor of religion, and he discoursed about holiness. "That sounds to me like the religion of the Bible, and if I could only see such religion carried out in the lives of those who profess to believe the Bible, I would surely give up my infidelity," said Mrs. P___. She soon found that there were those who by their lives exemplified all they professed, and became established in the truth of the Christian religion. It was but a short time afterward that she was brought to experience its renovating influences. About three or four months she continued, though a lamb of the fold, to company with those who had taken the higher walk of the Christian, and one day when at the Tuesday meeting, while the way of faith was being explained, by alluding to the example of Abraham, (Genesis xv,) she was enabled to bring the sacrifice of all her redeemed powers in obedience to the command of God, Rom. xii, 1. She judged him faithful who had promised, laid the offering upon the altar, and waited for the descent of the heavenly fire. This she was informed was the *Lord's* part of the work — the sacrifice was *his* property the moment it was laid upon the altar, and though the consuming fire might seem to tarry long, as in the case of Abraham, yet all she had to do was to keep the sacrifice upon the *Lord's* ALTAR, and, as the Lord's property, guard it from the touch of pollution. She did so, and with several others joined in singing the solemn words of the consecration hymn:-

"Lord, in the strength of grace,
With a glad heart and free,
Myself, my residue of days
I consecrate to thee.

"Thy ransomed servant, I,
Restore to thee thine own;
And from this moment, live or die,
To serve my God alone."

The covenant was ratified in heaven, and from that hour she was enabled to testify, unwaveringly, of the blessedness of a state of holiness. On the succeeding Thursday afternoon, at class meeting, she desired me to give the illustration of the way of faith which had been given on Tuesday. She had brought with her a friend, who had been won from the ranks of infidelity to the cross of Christ, through her instrumentality, and she greatly desired her friend should see the simplicity of the way of holiness. I endeavored to present it in a similar manner, and Mrs. F. was also enabled to lay her all upon the altar, and believe God, and ever since has been enabled to bring forth the fruits of holiness. From these dear Christian friends the blessed heritage of the believer has not been withheld: "Unto them it has been given in behalf of Christ, not only to believe on his name, but also to *suffer* for his sake." Few could with greater propriety say, "The Lord requires so much faith of me." Diversified trials have assailed them: "the rain descended, the floods came, and the winds blew," and in the midst of all they have stood, incontrovertibly evidencing the blessedness of the assurance, that "it is a good thing that the heart be established with grace." had their friends yielded to the mistaken idea that the doctrine of holiness is too strong meat for *babes* in Christ, these individuals would doubtless, during their early experience, have remained comparatively uninstructed in the doctrine of holiness, and when assailed by these storms of persecution, little probability remains but that the superstructure of their religious profession would have fallen, to the triumph of infidelity.

These dear friends cannot now conceive of the requirements of the Bible being answered in anything less than holiness. And they think of conversion as a point in experience, from which the believer is required by the word to go forward directly into the promised land — the rest of faith. Soon after Mrs. P___'s conversion, she brought her father to a meeting where testimony on the experience of holiness was the absorbing topic. Over sixty years he had lived in infidelity, but from the testimony that evening adduced, he became a convert to Christianity, and shortly afterward resigned himself wholly to Christ, and has since eminently adorned the doctrine of God his Savior. One could hardly forbear thinking of a Carvosso in witnessing his whole-heartedness in the cause of his Redeemer. (Note: He has since gone moat triumphantly home to heaven, witnessing, to the last, the excellency of holiness.)

A sister of Mrs. P___ also, who had become settled in the principles of infidelity, from the, idea that Christians do not really believe what they profess, was also brought to the Tuesday and Saturday night meetings, and from an exhibition of what she had conceived *Bible* religion demanded, she also gave up her infidelity, (for which she had for years been quite a champion,) and soon experienced religion. But her mind was fully purposed on nothing less than full salvation from all sin. She was brought most understandingly and interestingly into the enjoyment of the witness of holiness, and has since, with her sister, been very instrumental in bringing others into the way. Had not holiness been presented as a Bible doctrine to these individuals, even when in their *unconverted* state, they would have remained infidels. And they *became* infidels by not seeing holiness carried out in the lives of professors. What a lesson do these cases furnish to those who consider holiness such a *high* doctrine of our creed, that they but seldom, in their ministrations, present it! And how admonitory to *unholy* professors also! Alas! how many such have been the means of making infidels!

O how needful that judgment begin at the house of God, relative to this subject! Mr. Wesley apprehended its importance perhaps more fully than some of his sons in the gospel, as his last advice most clearly exhibits. It reads thus: "*Therefore, all our preachers should make a point of preaching per-*

fection to believers, constantly — strongly — and explicitly, and all believers should mind this one thing, and continually agonize for it."

December 24. The circumstances of my health of late have led me to think much about exchanging worlds. I rejoice to say I can look to the future, without fearful forebodings. What a victory hath grace gained! A few years since, when in similar circumstances, how dissimilar was my experience! A consciousness that I had not been wholly devoted to God, and had not made the purposes of life subservient to the one great object of laying up treasure in heaven, made everything relative to the future appear dismal. When the trial came, and I was so extremely ill that my life was despaired of, O, with what inexpressible regret did I look back upon the history of my life! I thought of the abundant entrance that might have been administered unto me into the everlasting kingdom of our Lord and Savior Jesus Christ. As I heard a little girl crying "Blackberries for sale," passing my window I thought how gladly would I live, though it were only to be as that little girl, so that I might say beseechingly to each passing stranger, "Love my Jesus!" But who will thank the Lord that I have lived? 'What have I done toward helping others to heaven?' There was but one thing that I could with satisfaction contemplate; and that was just what the enemy had tempted me most sorely about when in health. I had ever felt that if I had a talent to be in the least degree useful by the way of writing, that God required the use of it in his own service, and to use it otherwise would be *desecration*. When I tried to devote the talent to the service of Christ, the accuser suggested that what I had written was deceptive, and bespoke a higher state of piety than my attainments would warrant.

Now, when so near the eternal world that the light of eternity beamed upon my mind, I was given to see every little act or circumstance of my life tremendously important. I beheld the minutiae of my existence gathered up into one mighty whole — acting upon the mass of mind on which I had been surrounded, and witnessed it spreading into wider, and yet wider circles; and then rolling down through the ages of time, until the final hour when the judgment should set, and the books be opened.

I had a faint hope of salvation through the Savior of sinners. But the idea of being *barely* saved, when an abundant entrance might have been ministered unto me, and of having done so little for Christ when there had been so much to do, was revolting to my feelings, and made heaven appear not so much a matter of anticipation as one would imagine. Often have I since felt that I would love to be a living epistle to the many who are willing to be *barely* saved. Doubtless many such will be *just* lost!

A striking illustration of what I would say was furnished in the case of a young lady, who began well. With much pain, I had noticed that she had ceased to be a *cross-bearing* Christian. I had through Christ begotten her in the gospel, and, with unutterable yearnings, I expostulated with her relative to the importance of endeavoring to be useful. She treated my importunity lightly, and said, "I think I shall do well if I but make out to save my own soul."

"God *requires* you should be useful, and has not left the matter optional with yourself, and if you aim only at saving your own soul, you will not only lose your precious soul, but will doubtless be influential, through your evil example as a professor, in influencing other spirits, which will be lost, and thus, instead of laying up treasure in heaven, you will be treasuring up wrath against the day of wrath."

She concluded that there were so many that seemed to get on *without* whole-heartedness in the cause, that she would risk the matter, and soon became a trifling, worldly-minded professor, and yet, with thousands like herself, seems to fancy herself on the way to heaven. O, what terrible disappointments will such meet with at last, when, after having been ferried by Vain-hope over the stream of Death, they come up to the gate of heaven, and say, Lord! Lord! open unto us.

I too might have been of the number, had not grace interposed. But now, in view of exchanging worlds, blissful hopes of immortality and eternal life open before me. To God be *all* the glory!

February 26. While I write, the remains of the beloved President Fisk are probably being borne to the house appointed for all living. At 10 o'clock this morning his friends assemble to take their last leave of his almost sainted form.

"To know him was to love."

In the early part of his Christian career he was enabled to discern the mark of the prize of his high calling, and became an earnest seeker after full salvation. He did not conceive the dignity of the ministry lowered by acknowledging, before a band of devoted brethren and sisters, his need of holiness as an essential qualification for his holy calling. Having enlisted the prayerful sympathies of a little chosen band, he bowed as an humble seeker after this pearl of great price. Had he been less importunate, and remained indefinite in his acknowledgments and petitions, he would probably never have been a *witness* of perfect love. In succeeding years, all his ministrations, and even his very person, seemed to exhibit the beauty of holiness. Could he now speak, he would doubtless refer to a little camp-meeting scene, where, secluded from the eye of the world, with a little company of disciples, he came out in definite acknowledgment, in pursuit of holiness, as the period when the foundation was laid, from whence emanated mainly his superior excellence.

Weariness of the flesh, and wakeful nights, have for some time past been appointed me. But God is my witness that I have not a wish apart from his will, -

"I will suffer, and fulfill
All my Savior's righteous will;

Be in all alike resign'd,
Jesus was a patient mind."

It is the will of my heavenly Father that patience should have its perfect work, so that I may be perfect and entire, wanting nothing. And when he takes his own way to accomplish it, shall I not rejoice! Yes, blessed be the Lord, my strength, I will rejoice in tribulation! The trial of my faith is *precious*.

The spiritual world seems very near. On hearing of the departure of the beloved Fisk, my spirit seemed to follow his flight, and the idea of being permitted to greet him in the abodes of immortality, within perhaps a few short weeks, does not seem improbable. On hearing of his transition from earth to heaven, during the wakefulness of the succeeding night, my mind thus memorialized its imaginings in verse

>Two spirits met;
One was dismantled, and was from the clime
Where dwell the just, who pass the bounds of time,
>And earthly pangs forget;
"And know'st thou not," said he with joyous air,
(To one who had not pass'd earth's bounds of care,)
>"That this is a high day?
And that our realms are ringing with delight?
For lo! an heir of heaven — a child of light,
Borne through the ethereal way,
Came to the joyous presence of our King,
And now through all our blissful realms doth ring,
>A greeting welcome lay."
But ah! a pall that told of much despair,
Hung, curtain-like, around that child of care,
>As weepingly he said,
"And know'st thou not, that earth doth deeply mourn?
That while thou joyest for a seraph born,
Earth mourns a champion dead?
He was a burning light, faith fed the blaze,
And though we gloried in the lucent rays,.
>As from heaven's altar lent;
And knew from whence it came — from whence it burn'd:
And that it would be to its source return'd.
Yet its extinguishment
On earth we mourn: 'tis thus that in one day
Ye sing a seraph born, and we a weeping lay."

>Thus heaven hath sympathies,
Pure, constant, fresh-born — every moment new,

And earth hath fresh-born, ever-varying sorrows too,
    And signal'd much as these:
But faith — strong, mighty faith, can plume the wing,
And mortals too, in seraph chorus sing
    With those of heavenly birth;
For keen-eyed faith dismantles the disguise,
Which, speaks a want of one-like sympathies
    Between sweet heaven and earth.

April 16. The birthday of my little S___. She has now been spared to us six years. have sometimes thought that our heavenly Father has taken special pains to teach us, that our little ones are not our own.

I shall never forget the feelings with which I received my dear S___ from the hand of the Lord. Two precious boys had previously been removed to the heavenly fold. The reason why they were taken had been written enduringly upon my heart. And now, on our little S___ being intrusted, the Holy Spirit was true to its work on my heart, in causing the memory of the past to come up vividly before me.

The duty of consecrating our children to God in the holy ordinance of baptism was clear to my mind; but the responsibility I should thereby bring upon myself, caused me from week to week to delay this act of consecration with our first-born; little adornments, requiring, as I feared, a useless expenditure of time and expense, were indulged in, and I waited to feel a perfect clearness relative to the fact that I *really* gave him up, *body,* as well as soul, to God.

With thousands of mothers, I had spent hours of precious time in embroidering his garments; hours, which, as they winged their report to eternity, had left traces of painful uncertainty upon my mind, that I *might* be wrong.

"If I give up this child in baptism, I virtually take upon myself the acknowledgment that he is the *Lord's,* and if the *Lord's,* should I adorn him thus?" It was thus I reasoned, and (while lingering from week to week) God suddenly took our first-born to himself.

The pangs that followed were severe indeed; probably tenfold more so than if the matter of giving him up to God had been previously decided. I felt that he was *taken* away — not *given* up — *torn* from my embrace — not a *free-will offering.*

I did not forget the admonition entirely, and strange that a lesson so painful should not fully accomplish the purpose whereunto it was sent. But I had not yet experimentally apprehended the admonitions: "Thou shalt have no other gods before me:" "I the Lord your God am a *jealous* God."

When our heavenly Father intrusted us with another heir of immortality, I did not err precisely on the same ground, but I looked abroad on the manner in which I had been accustomed to make myself useful, beyond the immediate limits of my family, and, with an unwarrantable complacency of feeling, said in my heart, "Now that God has made up my loss, I will *live* for this one dear object — I will have done with those more extended expectations, and absorb my mind's energies in this beloved one." "I am fearful if the Lord should take that little one away, that you would not be willing to let it go," said my beloved husband, almost chidingly, on observing the inordinate absorption of my love. "I do not feel as if God would take him," I replied: "he has given him to replace the loss of the other." The idea of losing him no more entered into my contemplations than if it were impossible. He appeared perfectly healthy when these observations were made, but in about one short week his sweet spirit passed from earth, and we were again childless.

Dear S___ , whose sixth birthday I now commemorate, was the next we were permitted to embrace. I shall never forget the chastened feelings with which I first looked upon this beloved one. My heart seemed to be perfectly subdued, and I indeed received her as a precious loan. And now my beloved husband and myself are fully united in purpose, in endeavoring to bring her up for the Lord. We hear his word authoritatively saying to us, *"Take this child, and nurse it for me!"* Should an earthly potentate say, "Take this child, and nurse it for *me*," what vigilance would be necessary! How many observers to report the matter in every minutiae if unfaithful to the trust committed! But now that the King of kings — the Lord of lords — intrusts a candidate for an immortal crown! — now that an innumerable company of invisible intelligences — ay, greatly-interested and divinely-authorized agencies ("For their angels do always behold the face of my Father") are beholding us, O, with what circumspection should this heir of immortality be trained!

Little S has often evinced, most decisively, that the Holy Spirit measurably influences her heart. On an occasion about two years since, I left her after having seen her, as I supposed, quietly sinking to repose; the usual devotions of the evening had been performed, and I retired to another room. Some time afterward, I heard a subdued sobbing, and on going to her, to my astonishment, found that she had been weeping bitterly.

"O, ma," she exclaimed, *"I want to pray!"* On telling her how much the Savior loved little children, and that he had said," Suffer little children to come unto me," with great eagerness she caught the words ere I had finished, and rejoicingly, amid her tears, exclaimed, "And forbid them not, for of such is the kingdom of heaven!" After this, her mourning was ended, and gladness and love filled her soul. She seemed to feel satisfied that the Savior had received her.

For some time previous to this we had been much in prayer for the salvation of her soul, and had conversed with her on the nature and necessity of a change of heart: and though we may not pronounce decidedly on the extent of this work, we feel that we can rejoice most assuringly in the confidence, that the Savior is wooing her to the embrace of his love, enough to encourage us greatly for future effort in her behalf.

May 17. Since I last noted my experience, I have been permitted to prove the all-sufficiency of grace to sustain in view of immediate dissolution. On the third day after my illness commenced, I was again, as on a former occasion, when in similar circumstances, taken with the puerperal fever; added to which the spasmodic rheumatism set in. "Grace is sufficient to sustain under all circumstances," had been a favorite expression with me. And now I was called to test whether it was sufficient to sustain in agonizing pain, and in view of a speedy departure from earth.

For hours I was not able to breathe without the greatest difficulty. In broken accents I said to a beloved one who was standing over me, *"I know whom I have believed!"* Had I been able to speak volumes, it seemed to me as if they could not have spoken more comprehensively than this one short expression of confidence.

At this point, it was suggested, "If raising your hand would decide the point, whether for life or death, would you dare lift it? I felt that I would not, so fully was I assured that the Judge of all the earth would do right. "But are you not being *cut* off in the midst of your days and usefulness?" was suggested. "I commit this with my other interests into the hands of the Lord. I have often asked, sooner than to be permitted to live, and dishonor in any way the profession I have made, of entire devotedness, the work might be cut short in righteousness and I taken home to heaven; and my heavenly Father may see me about to be overtaken by some extraordinary trial, in which my faith might fail, and in his tender love he may now be taking me from the evil to come," I replied. I looked upon the many ties calculated to bind me to earth — upon the one next to God nearest my heart — my precious little ones, and the many beloved friends who would love to detain me, and thought of a misanthropic expression of infidelity, "that it is but little to die, when one has nothing to live for;" and my heart exclaimed, "Thanks be to God who giveth me the victory through our Lord Jesus Christ." For notwithstanding my nature was far from being insensible to the many endearments which would have invited a longer stay on earth, I still felt if worlds were offered as an inducement to decide the point, whether to live or die, I would not dare choose. My whole soul in humble acquiescence said, "Good is the will of the Lord!"

While thus for hours lingering between life and death, so indescribably important did holiness appear, that I thought if abiding in the flesh to labor for God till a pilgrimage of threescore years were accomplished, and the whole amount of service during that lengthened detainment from the joys of the upper world, should only result in inducing *one* worldly-minded professor to be whole-hearted in the service of Christ, I should be richly repaid.

Previous to my severe illness, in my endeavors to grasp an object of faith definitely, I had frequently been subjected to such severe mental effort, that my nature had often been much wearied in the exercise. Sometimes I had been left to contend, to what seemed to be the last point of endurance, and then

"When my all of strength has fail'd,
I have with the God-man prevail'd,"

by just getting hold (as Fletcher says) of the last link of the chain, "He will fulfill the desire of them that fear him." "When your physical frame becomes enfeebled by disease, and your mental capacities become enervated, in sympathy with your physical frame, then you will be unable to withstand, and you may expect great perplexities," said the accuser. This temptation had led me to pray much, prior to my illness, for grace to sustain, in such a manner that God might in the highest degree be glorified, should I become thus enfeebled; and lo! instead of being withstood by the evil one, I had peace within all my borders, and seemed to have little more to do with the powers of darkness, than if I had been already translated from earth to heaven.

After remaining several hours in a very critical state, it was urged upon my mind, "All are yours, whether life or death:" "Ask what you will, and it shall be done unto you:" — it will be according to the will of God. For a short time I partially resisted the influence from the consideration that nature clings to life. It was not without trying the Spirit, with most careful vigilance, by "the law and the testimony," that I yielded to its influence. I thought of that state where, after millions on millions of ages have passed, my felicities would be but begun, and of the thousands of unholy professors, unprepared for its beatitudes, and yet, almost unconscious of their unpreparedness, and unalarmed about their unfitness; and I felt that I could forego the felicities of heaven for many long years of sojourning below, if I could in any way be helpful toward arousing one of this description to the importance of holiness as a *necessary* qualification for heaven, and could wish to live if it were for this only, if fully assured it were according to the will of God.

"Ask what you *will,* and it will be according to the will of God," was again urged. And then there was one to whom I had been united *in the Lord.* I thought of his peculiar temperament, and the manner in which we had been permitted to be helpful to each other, and his loneliness amid the buffetings of the world, and of our little ones who were to be trained for immortality, and again said, "If I knew it were according to the will of God, I could ask life for their sake, and again it was repeated yet more impressively, "Ask what you will — all are yours — choose either life or death, and it will be according to the will of God."

I dared not resist longer: and said, "O Lord, I am thine! I live but to glorify thee; renewedly I commit my whole being into thy hands — body, soul, and spirit, time, talents, and influence, I again, in most entire surrender, consecrate to thee. If it be but to glorify thee, *let me live!* but if thou seest me at any time about to dishonor the cause of holiness, by ceasing to be wholly devoted to thy service, cut short the work in righteousness, and take me home to thyself." At once I felt that I should recover. All the alarming symptoms were with amazing rapidity removed, and for some time past I have been permitted to go in and out before my family, and to enjoy the services of the sanctuary.

And now, with all my heart, do I praise my covenant-keeping God for the lengthened trial through which I have passed. I used to say that "grace is sufficient to sustain under all circumstances," because I knew it. Now I can say, it is sufficient to sustain fully, and even in a joyous state of mind amid agonizing pain, and also in full view of the "king of terrors." Glory be to God in the highest, and let everything that hath breath praise the Lord!

June 21. On Wednesday evening I attended the anniversary of the Juvenile Missionary Society. Many humorsome tales were told by one of the speakers, illustrative of the spirit prevailing in the west in behalf of missions. By the merriment induced, I could not but question the expediency of provoking so much lightness. Yet the Lord condescended to cause the trial to work together for my good.

It was stated that on account of the scarcity of money at the west, one presented a young colt, which was kept with much care, until suitable for missionary service. A pious man, having nothing at his own disposal but his person, offered *himself:* upon inquiry, he was found a suitable person, and in due time, both the horse, with the man who had offered himself as the rider, were off on missionary ground. Another presented the produce of a specified piece of ground, and with much care cultivated it. At the close of the season, he was able to make an offering by no means small for the cause of missions. Another offered a small pig, and the humorsome details were given as to the care with which it was nourished, and the deep interest of the community about "the missionary pig."

Considering the extreme lightness occasioned, I felt that the matter was indeed exceedingly dubious; yet I knew my heavenly Father could overrule it for my good, and I was enabled to claim the assurance that it should be so. I began to ask, What more can I devote to the cause of God? I felt that my person and property, my all, were already his, and with a longing desire to know, I earnestly inquired of God whether there was anything within my reach that might be *specially* set apart for his service. Most unexpectedly, an object before unthought of was presented with vividness to my mind. "There is that little daughter lately intrusted to your keeping; are you willing to set her apart in a *special* manner for this cause, or any other self-denying duties to which God may appoint her?" I was startled, and a train of reflections followed, which can never be forgotten. I saw the responsibilities of a perpetual vow to train her with an exclusive view to usefulness in the vineyard of the Lord as indeed important. For a moment I was tempted to leave the matter in indefiniteness, but I remembered that I had asked the Lord to direct my mind, and now that he had pointed to the object, I felt that I would not withhold her, and with a solemnity of spirit, never to be forgotten, I laid the sacrifice upon the altar.

After I had made the offering, a *realization* of its acceptance was given, and, in view of the exceeding propriety of the act, I rejoiced that my heavenly Father had moved me to it.

"But will you train one with a special view to the self-denying service of God, and not take similar obligations upon yourself relative to the other?" said the Holy Spirit, appealingly. And now in reference to the elder and only remaining child, I am sure the Lord helped me to count the cost. I never before discovered, so clearly, the difference between training a child up for the world, or with a special view to the self-sacrificing service of Christ; but after weighing it in its proper bearings, I, through grace, made the surrender, and *felt* that the offering was accepted.

The next morning I said to the elder of the two, "S___, I was at a missionary meeting last night, and heard several good — true stories." She sat down, deeply interested, and I began to relate, circumstantially, the story about the horse and his rider, the ground, &c. She was interested, even beyond my expectation. After I had finished the recital, I said, in a manner calculated to excite her curiosity, — "Ma gave something too; what do you think it was, my daughter?"

"Why, your heart!"

"Yes, I gave my heart; but I gave that a long time since, and I keep giving — *giving it all the time;* but I also gave something else, and what do you think it could have been?" I desired to raise her curiosity to the highest point, and the Lord favored my effort.

She began to enumerate everything she could imagine, and then gave up in discouragement, and said, "I *cannot* tell; please, ma, *do* tell me?"

I paused, and, in an impressive manner, said, "Why, I gave *you* and your little sister." Her color changed, and, in consternation, she exclaimed, — "Why, ma?"

I felt that the Lord was peculiarly owning my effort; and I can hardly describe my emotions of praise, wonder, and love. I continued to say, "Yes, my daughter, I gave *you* and your little sister to the Lord; and now, perhaps, he will let me keep you a little while, to bring you up for *him*. I must not permit you to do anything but what the Lord would love to have you do. And now I do not mean to have you learn anything but just what I think the Lord would love to have you learn. When I dress you, I mean to think whether the Lord would love to have my daughter wear such things; and in *everything* I do for you, I must do it in view of bringing you up for God. You must ever remember that you belong to him, and never do anything but what you think he would love to have you do.

The Holy Spirit directed the effort, and her young heart apprehends, in a manner beyond her former conception, the truth that she, in reality, belongs to God. Since, when reproof has been necessary, I have said, "S___ , I think the Lord would not love to have you do thus or so," and it has been sufficient. And never before have I so deeply realized my responsibility as a mother.

July 4. What a scene have I this day witnessed! At eleven o'clock this morning I went with the intention of staying but a short season, to mingle in the joyousness of a Sunday-school celebration on Staten Island. Returning home this afternoon, an immense crowd being on the boat, the upper deck gave, way, and crushed the multitude below. Two were killed instantly, and many were wounded. My husband had taken his carriage, and on account of the boat being so much crowded, we retained our seat in it, otherwise we would probably have been crushed with the multitude. As my husband passed amid the sufferers, endeavoring to administer relief, he heard one calling upon Jesus to come and take him unto himself.

"And do you feel that you have made your peace with God?" said my husband. "Yes, glory be to God," he replied, and continued to praise the Lord, with joyful lips, amid excruciating agonies. He appeared to be in dying circumstances. Who, in witnessing such a triumph of grace, could but feel that the religion of the Bible is beyond all price? Near him was a Jew, who also apparently had been fatally injured: such a countenance I hope never to look upon again. It has followed me ever since. His horrified and agonized look seemed to say to the heart of every beholder, that he was "without God or Christ in the world." It was by the special providence alluded to we were preserved. To God be all the glory!

"Be all my added life employ'd
Thine image in my soul to see."

July 27. Last evening was the anniversary of the most memorable period in my existence. I would ever memorialize the return of this eve, with special thanksgiving, as the eventful period when I was permitted, through the blood of the everlasting covenant, to cast anchor within the veil; since which I can testify that I have enjoyed deeper and more soul-transforming communion with God than I ever before had any conception of. I feel that I am indeed permitted, through the infinite merits of my Savior, to abide as in the inner sanctuary of the divine presence. Since the memorable hour in which I gave myself wholly away to Christ, he has kept me so fully, that I have not once been permitted to cast away my confidence. My soul rests consciously, and with an inexpressible degree of assurance, upon the immutable word.

"Through unbelief I stagger not."

Praise the Lord, it is not in vain that I have trusted in Jesus! He not only saves me from sin, but he permits me to rely upon him as my wisdom. Never, in former experience, did I so deeply and habitually realize my utter destitution of every good thing *out* of Christ, but in Christ I feel that I *have* all things. "I can do all things *through* Christ which *strengtheneth* me." How I used to shrink from the cross! Now I feel that I can even glory in bearing it after my divine Master. In former experience, I used to shrink from the knowledge of duty. Now I love to get very near to Jesus -under the direct rays of the Sun of righteousness, in order to discern duty clearly. When duty calls, or my heavenly Father says, "Who will go?" my heart quickly responds, "Here am I, send me!" O what a transformation hath grace made! "From this time it shall be said, What hath God wrought?"

August. During several days past, I have had great trials, and also great victories. Part of last week and the week before I spent at the grove, the most of my little family being with me. During the early part of the time, I was tempted that there was so much heartlessness in my exercises, that they were unprofitable to others, and but little benefit to myself. But when duty called, as it frequently did, I dared not resist, fearful it might be said, to the dishonor of the cause of holiness. "What do ye more than others?"

The enemy did not suggest that God had never called me to activity in the service of Christ, but he often tauntingly said, "Is not this want of liberty an assurance that you are not called to it *now?*" This continued till Sabbath evening. We then had an experience meeting in one of the large tents. I had been instrumental in getting the meeting together, and as I entered the tent it was suggested, "You surely will not be required to say much to-night, or the friends may think you convened the meeting for that purpose."

I was not at the moment aware that it was temptation, and thought the suggestion plausible. But though there were many dear friends present, yet there was a great want of ready witnesses for Jesus in the early part of the meeting. Notwithstanding the temptation, I *dared* not do otherwise than break in upon a pause which ensued, after the opening of the meeting. But I seemed not to have divine assistance. The powerful temptations which succeeded, for about an hour, baffle description. "Had not your previous exercises been sufficient to assure you that God is going to lay you by, in order to know whether you are willing to be *useless?*" was now urged.

To settle down in inactivity, when not disabled from mental or physical causes, could not, in my mind, be reconciled with the will of God. I could see nothing in the word of God that required I should be *willing to be useless,* but much that demanded *activity*. How to exemplify to the eye of beholders obedience to the demands, "Be ye steadfast, immovable, always abounding in the work of the Lord" — "instant in season, and out of season" — "lay up treasure in heaven," &c., and abide in inactivity, were questions which I could not resolve into the will of God. "It were better to be silent than to dishonor the cause, as you have done this evening," said the tempter. My mouth might have been closed, but my resolution was fixed, rather to die in the conflict, than that the enemy should have even a partial triumph. It was doubtless the Holy Spirit that urged upon my mind to ask, if I had not really dishonored the cause by speaking, that the brother in charge might be induced to call upon me to pray at the close of the meeting. I had hardly made the request, before our venerable father Smith said, "Sister____ will now close the meeting with prayer." The snare was broken, and glorious liberty succeeded.

"Did you ever hear me attempt to speak when there was such a manifest want of liberty, as at the commencement of this meeting?' said I to a devoted friend at the close of the exercises. She looked astonished, and said "Why never in my life have I heard you speak with greater liberty!" As I had been similarly influenced relative to the exercises during several preceding days, I began to conceive that it might all have been temptation, and I said to my beloved sister S____, "You may have noticed the restraint I have been laboring under for days, which has induced me to limit my labor to positive exigencies, and this only because I have not *dared* to refuse!"

"My own mind has been in the same state precisely," said she, and the want of liberty I had felt in exercising, disposed me to feel like throwing the labor on you, from the idea that you had more than usual liberty. Sister S____ in saying what she did, relative to me, had fully described *my* views relative to *her,* and now the temptation with both was broken. During the remainder of our stay on the encampment, I was blessed with greater liberty of spirit than I had ever before enjoyed. I was given to feel that it was indeed high honor conferred on mortals, to be *permitted* to say one word in honor of Christ, or to do anything, however small, calculated to advance the interests of the Redeemer's kingdom.

The concerns of my little family demanded much of my attention; but whenever a few moments for social worship could be obtained, I was enabled to be in the Spirit, and though much exposed to care, my Savior saved me from it. Praise his name!

Sabbath evening, June 29, 18__. Memorable period! I am at a loss for language wherewith to record the abundant joy of my heart. On the evening of this date, my beloved S___, received clear witness of adoption into the family of Christ.

For some time past she has manifested increasing interest in spiritual things. She has also been more successful in governing her disposition, which is naturally very resolute. When, at times, it has gained the ascendency, and I have endeavored to show her how unlovely and sinful the indulgence of wrong tempers is in the sight of God, she has wept and prayed for forgiveness, and earnestly asked for a heart which would incline her to everything lovely and pure in the sight of God and man.

On Sabbath evening, previous to going with her to her room, I had an unusually sweet season in waiting before the Lord. It was necessary I should remain at home, but I had not settled in my contemplations the manner of spending the evening. In seeking for direction, I asked that the Lord would so take the lead of my mind, and all connecting circumstances, that the evening might be remembered in time, and eternity, as one of the most important in my Christian history.

I shall never forget the request, for it required such a struggle of faith to claim the assurance that I had the petition I had desired of God. Satan withstood with the suggestion, that there was no *reasonable* foundation for the fulfillment of such an expectation. Human probabilities were all against the indulgence of the idea of anything unusual, and why should I imagine that God would condescend to go out of his ordinary way of working, when there was nothing in the intimation of existing circumstances to warrant such an expectation? But the Holy Spirit said, "*All* things are possible with God, and all things are possible to him that *believeth*." With this I was strengthened to claim the assurance that the desire of my heart should be granted. But I did not receive at the time the least intimation of the manner in which God would prove his faithfulness.

Soon afterward, I accompanied my daughter to her room, and before assisting her to undress, I read to her an interesting account of little Mary P. Clark, from the Christian Advocate and Journal. She was much affected and exclaimed, - "What a sweet good child she must have been!"

"Mary must have had a new heart, or she could not have been such a sweet good child," I observed. "And you may be sure, dear S___, that the Lord is just as willing to give you a new heart as he was to bestow such a precious gift upon Mary.

"O! I *wish* I had it! O, I want it *now!*" she exclaimed with increasing emotion.

"Well, your heavenly Father wants to give it to you now, my dear daughter. He says, '*Ask* and you *shall* receive.' 'Come unto *me;*' and he wants you to come unto him *now.* He is saying to you this moment, 'Try me, and prove me.' Now, try the Lord, and prove him. See if he will not give you a new heart. That heart of yours *already* belongs to God, and now as he requires it of you, will he not take it? He just now says, *'Give* me thy heart.' You well know how it would be, should you ask your mother for anything which she knew to be for your good. Would she not give it to you? And now how *much more* willing is your heavenly Father to give the Holy Spirit to them that *ask* him? He knows you *need* a new heart, and he only waits for *you* to come to him, and ask, and you *shall* receive.

"We will now kneel, and ask that God will receive you, and while you give yourself away to him, we will beseech him to give you a new heart."

With looks expressive of unutterable desire she assented, and we knelt together. I endeavored to be mouth for her in confessing her need of a Savior, and in earnest supplication for pardon and adoption. Her fervent responses spoke assuringly to my heart, as, in verity, the language of her overburdened spirit. I felt, most consciously, that I beheld in her experience the significant expression verified, "The Spirit maketh intercession with groanings unutterable." The great deep of her heart seemed broken up, and the violence of her grief was so great, that I was fearful the excitement might prevent that calm, decisive action of faith, by which the soul throws itself on the mercy of God, through our Lord Jesus Christ.

Yet, notwithstanding this, I felt so desirous that every step should be distinctly marked with the most incontestable evidence of the Holy Spirit's leadings, both for the establishment of my own faith, and the permanency of hers, that I resolved, though my nature shrank from being instrumental in probing her wounded spirit more deeply, to continue my efforts yet a little longer in endeavoring to discover to her a more thorough knowledge of her need of a Savior.

We had risen from prayer, and I said, "Did you ever think, dear S___, that all the sins you ever committed were written down in the book of the Lord?" I then told her of a youthful relative, who, a few moments previous to his death, repeated the hymn

> Almighty God! thy piercing eye
>   Strikes through the shades of night,
> And our most secret actions lie
>   All open to thy sight.
>
> There's not a sin which we commit,
>   Or wicked word we say,
> But in that dreadful book is writ,
>   Against the judgment day.
>
> And must the sins which I have done
>   Be read and published there?
> Be all exposed before the Son,
>   While men and angels hear?
>
> Lord, at thy feet ashamed I lie;
>   Upward I dare not look;
> Pardon my sins before I die,
>   And blot them from thy book.

The effect produced on her mind while repeating these lines I can never forget. The Lord was eminently present, and spoke, through the medium of the words, to her inmost heart. As I progressed, her emotions were increasingly demonstrative of the fact, that she felt herself standing, as a condemned criminal, before God. And when I came to the last stanza, the language of her quivering spirit seemed to say, "Spare, I can bear no more."

Never before, for other than my own soul, had I felt such a weight of responsibility. It was in part induced from the conviction that it was the design of my heavenly Father, that the conversion of my dear child might depend, instrumentally, upon the strength of my faith. The unutterable solicitude educed from this conviction, influenced me to pause, in prayerful suspense, before the Lord. Her spirit seemed almost overwhelmed; and O, with what longing of soul did I wait for heavenly direction!

She knelt for the performance of her evening's devotion, during the continuance of this waiting suspense with myself. Her unusual fervor and tone of voice seemed to say, that she was quite unconscious of the presence of any one besides the God whom she supplicated. After continuing much longer than usual in prayer, she arose, and was prepared for the repose of the night. But her fervor of spirit had not in the least abated. As she threw herself on the bed, she expressed her unwillingness to give up by saying, imploringly, "O! ma, keep talking to me."

I laid myself down beside her. O, the unutterable interest of that hour! I felt that her inmost soul was inexpressibly athirst for salvation. The conviction, with increasing certainty, possessed my heart, that she was about to be born of the Spirit. And who but a parent, similarly situated, could imagine feelings of like interest? That our child should thus, in her infant days, be born of the Spirit and adopted into the family of Christ! the honor seemed too great, and to grasp it seemed to require the exercise of a faith correspondingly greater.

It was but a short time before she was again in the attitude of a suppliant beside the bed. With my eye fixed upon Jesus, and my heart continually pleading the promise, "I will instruct thee," I endeavored to direct this precious lamb to the fold of Christ, by showing her the simplicity of the way of faith, while my own soul was every moment gathering increasing strength.

Soon afterward I said, "My daughter, I will pray silently, and you may also continue asking the Lord, and, O! I am sure he will give you a new heart." How sweet was the assurance to my soul, that the Holy Spirit would take of the things of God, and reveal them even unto babes. The sentiment, "Not by might nor by power, but by my Spirit, saith the Lord," never more thoroughly penetrated my heart. There was one point in my travail of soul for her, where my faith most consciously laid hold. It was while saying, "She is already thine;" and now, by the remembrance of that hour, when she was most solemnly given away in covenant to thee, and thou didst condescend to assure my heart so fully of thine acceptance of the offering, let her case come up in remembrance before thee. Thus far she *is already* thine — numbered with thy covenant people; and now wilt thou not give *her* to feel most assuredly that she is taken into covenant relation with thee? May her young heart know that thou dost accept and seal her thine.

It was while thus pleading that my faith most *distinctly* laid hold. I pause here; for here is the burden of my heart in the recordings of this hour. God is a covenant-keeping God. His name is JEHOVAH. And by this name would he now be known and glorified in his covenant people, and their seed after them. A solemn, unfathomed responsibility rests upon God's chosen ones relative to their children. Of this I had never been so fully aware, until passing through the exercises here given.

She is *already* thine! Here was the point where my faith, with an unyielding grasp, laid hold. It was here my bounding spirit could say,

> "My prayer hath power with God; the grace
>   Unspeakable I now receive."

So sure was I now that what I had asked was according to the will of God, and that I had the petition I had desired of him, that I continued a moment longer, praising God for the answer, though my heart assured me that my dear child was longing for me to rise in order to communicate her joy.

As I arose, she exclaimed, with thrilling emotion, "O, ma, I feel as if I had a new heart! O, I think I have! I am almost sure! O, I *am* sure! Yes, *I am sure!*" She then began praising the Lord, with expressions altogether beyond her former capacity. I could not but regard her singularly mature expressions, so beyond her former self, as a development of renewed mental powers. A new nature had been given, and my condescending heavenly Father permitted me to have such conclusive testimony that my heart may ever say, relative to her change, -

"Meridian evidence puts doubt to flight."

"O, praise the Lord!" was for some time the language of every breath. "How truly the heaven-inspired language of the new-born spirit!" thought I, as I listened to one but little over six years of age, who was unaccustomed to mingle with those similarly exercised with herself.

From one expression I had reason to conclude that her mind had some time previously been exercised relative to this change. It was this: "O ma, how much I have of late thought of those words you published a long time ago!" "What were they, my daughter?" She quickly, and with much emphasis, replied, —

"'Give me thy heart!' we hear Him say;
Lord, we thy mandate will obey,
We come to tread the narrow way,
   To be thy faithful followers."

She then began to sing in sweet, and, I think, as lovely strains as ever I heard, to the tune of Old Hundred, the Doxology, -

"Praise God, from whom all blessings flow,
Praise him, all creatures here below;
Praise him above, ye heavenly host,
Praise Father, Son, and Holy Ghost

I accompanied her voice, with a heart bounding with unutterable joy. It really seemed to me that it was not in unmeaning, or unanswered invocation, that she had called upon the heavenly host to assist in ascribing praise to the Father, Son, and Holy Ghost. After she had ceased hymning the words, she returned, and, in solemn measure, said, "Yes!

"Praise God, from whom all blessings flow,
Praise him, all creatures here below;

Yes, everybody ought to praise him!" She paused, and then said, "O! I feel as if I wanted to tell everybody. O! I could tell a stranger. *Everybody* ought to love the Savior. I love him with my whole heart. O, how happy I am!"

We then united in singing portions of several hymns ascriptive of praise, in which she chose both the words and tunes, bearing me onward in heart and voice, though seemingly unconscious to herself, on the tide of her joy. She had commenced, and we had together sung,

"My Father, God! I feel, I feel thy love," &c.

As we sung, she emphasized the words most expressive of the language of her heart, and then said, "O, ma, there is one verse of that hymn so sweet to me now!" I repeated the first lines of the second stanza, inquiringly.

"That is not it.!' I then repeated the remaining lines:

"To hear him whisper, Thou art mine,
And all in me, my child, is thine,'
O! these are triumphs all divine."

"*That* is it! *O, what triumphs!*" she exclaimed.

She had never been a child in whom abundant precocity of sentiment had been manifested, as is in some rare cases, and I desire not to account for this maturity of experience and sentiment on any other ground than that of the Holy Spirit's gracious dictations; and my spirit was sweetly and fully satisfied, and cried out, "It is enough!" "Out of the mouth of babes and sucklings, Thou hast ordained *strength*, because of thine enemies, that thou mightest still the avenger." The genuineness of the work was so apparent that the enemy was silenced, and no room left for future misgivings.

Her dear father was absent. But she was so desirous to communicate the joy of her newborn spirit to him, that I sent for him. My heart and eyes fill at the recollection of the scene when this happy father was permitted to clasp to his heart his rejoicing daughter — his newborn child. The remembrance of the day of her birth into the natural world bears but little comparison.

To witness the answer to what had been the increasing desire of his heart from the earliest existence of his child, O! this was happiness not to be described.

I thought well to explain to her how she might retain the blessing, and said, "Now, it was by giving your heart away to God that you received a new heart; and the only way to keep it is to keep giving." She caught the words from my lips, and said, "Yes, *keep giving it, giving it all the time.*"

About two hours had passed, and she again laid down for repose. I placed the light in a convenient position and laid down beside her, with the blessed Bible in my hand, and began turning over the leaves with the intention of selecting portions suited to her state. "What are you looking for, dear ma?"

"For something good," I responded. "O!" said she, "it is *all* good." While I read, the word of the Lord seemed to be sweet indeed to her taste.

After reading for some time, and she had ceased to respond, I supposed she had fallen asleep, and ceased reading aloud "We love Him because he first loved us." She started up, and, with much interest, in "Why do you not read on, dear ma?" "Because I thought you had fallen asleep, or was sleepy." "O," said she, with much emphasis, "We love Him because he first loved us! We *did* not love him, but he loved us!"

It is now the third day since her change, and she still gives blessed evidence of its reality. She has always been very precious to us; but now, a new and yet more endearing tie binds her more closely to our hearts. Allelujah! The Lord God omnipotent reigneth!

www.ingramcontent.com/pod-product-compliance
Lightning Source LLC
Chambersburg PA
CBHW020011050426
42450CB00005B/417